INTERNATI
SOCIALIS

C000024902

A quarterly journal of socialist theory

ECONOMIC DEPRESSION now threatens to engulf the globe, confounding those who even a few months ago were insisting that it would be confined to South East Asia. In the first article of our special issue devoted to the analysis of this crisis Alex Callinicos charts the spread of the economic crash from its origins in South East Asia, through the collapse of the Russian economy to the threat now posed to the advanced Western economies. He goes on to assess the prospects which the new situation opens up for the global stability of the system. He concludes with an overview of the strategies available both to our rulers and to the working class movement internationally.

RUSSIA'S CATASTROPHE is qualitatively worse than virtually anything previously suffered by an advanced industrial economy in peacetime. Any thoughts that this judgement might be considered an exaggeration will be banished by Mike Haynes and Pete Glatter's forensic dissection of the Russian crisis. They show in revealing detail just what havoc has been wrought on the Russian society by its integration with the world market and analyse the decomposition of the Russian ruling class just at the point where it thought that it had successfully negotiated the transition from state capitalism.

'THIRD WORLD development' is rapidly becoming a contradiction in terms, as Phil Marfleet's analysis of globalisation and the Third World demonstrates. He looks at the claims of the boosters of globalisation and compares them with the real development of the world economy, concluding that Marxism, far from being outmoded by the expansion of the world market, has had its usefulness vindicated.

BOOK REVIEWS include Lindsey German's warm welcome for Ross McKibbin's *Class and Cultures: England 1918-1951*, Judy Cox on a new collection of John Reed's revolutionary journalism and Kevin Ovenden's appreciation of Ian Kershaw's biography of Hitler.

Editor: John Rees. Assistant editors: Alex Callinicos, Chris Harman, John Molyneux, Lindsey German, Colin Sparks, Mike Gonzalez, Peter Morgan, Mike Haynes, Judy Cox, Megan Trudell, Mark O'Brien, Rob Hoveman and Michael Lavalette.

Issue 81 of INTERNATIONAL SOCIALISM, quarterly journal of the Socialist Workers Party (Britain)

Published December 1998
Copyright © International Socialism
Distribution/subscriptions: International Socialism,
PO Box 82, London E3
American distribution: B de Boer, 113 East Center St, Nutley,
New Jersey 07110
Subscriptions and back copies: PO Box 16085, Chicago
Illinois 60616
Editorial and production: 0171 538 5821
Sales and subscriptions: 0171 538 5821
American sales: 773 665 7337

ISBN 1 898876 42 8

Printed by BPC Wheatons Ltd, Exeter, England
Typeset by East End Offset, London E3
Cover by Sherborne Design Ltd
Cover picture from Imagebank

For details of back copies see the end pages of this book

Subscription rates for one year (four issues) are:

Britain and overseas (surface):	individual	£14 ($30)
	institutional	£25
Air speeded supplement:	North America	£3
	Europe/South America	£3
	elsewhere	£4

Note to contributors

The deadline for articles intended for issue 82 of *International Socialism* is 22 January 1999

All contributions should be double-spaced with wide margins. Please submit two copies. If you write your contribution using a computer, please also supply a disk, together with details of the computer and programme used.

A quarterly journal of socialist theory

Winter 1998
Contents

Editorial

World capitalism at the abyss

ALEX CALLINICOS

In the past few months the core zones of world capitalism—the United States and the European Union—have suddenly found themselves peering over an economic abyss. The financial and governmental collapse in Russia in late August dramatised the fact that the crisis which had begun in East Asia in the summer of 1997 was spreading and threatening to engulf the entire global economy. The Hungarian-American speculator George Soros summed up the mood of panic that swept the world's financial centres in the autumn of 1998 when he told the US Congress, 'The global capitalist system that has been responsible for such remarkable prosperity is coming apart at the seams'.[1]

Coming as it does towards the end of a decade in which global financial markets have been dominated by an atmosphere of euphoria and greed and in which the official left has largely abandoned any intention of reforming capitalism, this unfolding crisis is a development of historic significance. Properly to grasp its nature requires that we understand that it has three distinct, but interrelated dimensions—the financial panic which seized the headlines, the behaviour of the underlying rate of profit, and the growing crisis of government policy. Let us consider these three dimensions in turn.

Financial panic

The Asian crash: Undeniably the crisis started in East Asia. Commentators talk constantly of 'financial contagion' and 'Asian flu', as if some mysterious disease is inexplicably spreading from Indonesia and South Korea to the rest of the world. In fact, the Asian crisis and the boom that preceded it can only be understood within the framework of the destabilising movements of money-capital on a global scale. US, Japanese and European speculators played a critical role in the entire process. The Asian crash is thus best seen as merely the first stage in the global economic crisis that is now unfolding rather than as a local upset that is somehow spilling over the rest of us.

As world capitalism celebrated the collapse of the Stalinist regimes during the first half of the 1990s, a huge surge of Western investment poured into the booming 'emerging markets' of East Asia and Latin America. This outflow of funds from the advanced economies was made possible by the growing integration of financial markets promoted by government policies of deregulation, which make it very easy to move money around the globe. In countries like South Korea, local capitalists gambled on their export markets continuing to grow at very high rates, and consequently made huge investments largely financed by foreign loans, often of a highly short term nature. As the boom reached fever pitch, investment became increasingly speculative, spilling into financial markets (in the process of being deregulated under pressure from Washington), real estate, and grandiose state projects (Malaysia's prime minister, Mahathir Mohamad, was particularly free spending).

The Asian boom helped to fuel a more general mood of confidence about the future of capitalism whose most visible feature was the extraordinary sustained rise of world stockmarkets in general, and of Wall Street in particular. Share prices soared against the background of a relatively mediocre performance by the big capitalist economies. In a series of perceptive leaders that appeared in December 1996, the leading capitalist paper, the *Financial Times,* surveyed this contradictory situation. 'Since 1990 the fastest annual rate of growth in real domestic product achieved by the OECD countries has been 2.7 percent,' the paper conceded. This compared unfavourably, not merely with the latter phase of the postwar boom in the 1960s and early 1970s (when European growth averaged 4.8 percent a year, US 4.3 percent, and Japanese 9.4 percent), but even with the crisis ridden 1970s and 1980s.

On this analysis government intervention would not achieve faster growth, since financial markets, having been badly burned by the great inflation of the 1970s and early 1980s, were deeply suspicious of anything that smacked of Keynesian demand management. The increased mobility of money-capital made possible by globally integrated markets meant that any state which appeared to be behaving 'imprudently' would suffer capital flight and a falling currency. The share boom offered a free market substitute for state intervention by providing a welcome stimulus to sluggish Western economies:

> *The joie de vivre on Wall Street may help to tide the world over to a more confident economic upturn in which the surprises may come on the side of faster than expected growth. This is, after all, a long cycle in which the contribution of the newly industrialising countries in Asia and elsewhere will be on an unprecedented scale.*[2]

On this analysis, dynamic East Asian capitalism represented the future of world capitalism, coming as it matured to the rescue of the stagnating advanced economies. In fact, the Asian boom was part of the problem, intimately linked to the booming financial markets in a pattern as old as capitalism. The economic historian Charles Kindelburger outlined the anatomy of the financial crises that have been an endemic feature of capitalism:

> *What happens, basically, is that some event changes the outlook. New opportunities for profit are seized, and overdone, in ways so closely resembling irrationality as to constitute a mania. Once the excessive character of the upswing is realised, the financial system experiences a sort of 'distress', in the course of which the rush to reverse the expansion process may become so precipitous as to resemble panic. In the manic phase, people of wealth or credit switch out of money or borrow to buy real or illiquid financial assets. In panic, the reverse movement takes place, from real or financial assets to money, or repayment of debt, with a crash in the prices of commodities, houses, buildings, land, stocks, bonds—in short, whatever has been the subject of the mania.*[3]

In the East Asian case it was the increasing problems faced by productive capital which precipitated the financial crash.[4] Competition for export markets became progressively more intense, especially after China devalued its currency, the renminbi, in 1994, and the Japanese yen began to fall against the US dollar from the spring of 1995 onwards. Most other East Asian currencies were pegged to the dollar, and therefore couldn't be devalued in response, so competition from cheaper Japanese and Chinese exports exerted increasing pressure throughout the region. Economies such as South Korea and Taiwan found themselves increasingly vulnerable to the fluctuations in the world price of the computer chips they export.

The result was massive over-investment and over-capacity in East Asia. The *Financial Times* summarised the conclusion of one study:

At an annual average growth rate of over 20 percent this decade, investment has been rising about three times as far as growth in domestic gross national product, suggesting Asia has been suffering from a serious case of over-investment. Now...capacity use is running at very low levels in countries such as China (below 60 percent), South Korea (below 70 percent) and Taiwan (72 percent).[5]

This gap between the underlying productive economy and the financial boom made a crash of some kind inevitable. Once confidence in East Asia began to crumble with the comparatively minor event of the collapse of the Thai currency, the baht, in July 1997, the huge investment boom unravelled astonishingly quickly. Speculators forced one East Asian currency after another off their pegs to the dollar. According to one study of the panic, it was local capitalists—Asian banks and corporations—who started selling off their currencies, but foreign investors soon joined in the rout.[6] Money poured out of East Asia as quickly as it had entered it in the first place. One commentator summarised the results:

The five countries that have been most damaged by the crisis—Indonesia, Malaysia, South Korea, Thailand and the Philippines—had net private inflows of $41 billion...in 1994. By 1996, this had jumped to $93 billion... Then, in 1997, came the panic: the net inflow turned into an estimated outflow of $12 billion. The swing in the net supply of private capital was $105 billion in just one year, a staggering 10 percent of the combined pre-crisis gross domestic product of the five countries.[7]

This massive flight of capital broke the backs of the worst affected economies. In order to get access again to foreign capital, their governments were forced to sign up to deals with the International Monetary Fund (IMF). The main thrust of the 'reform' programmes imposed as conditions of these 'rescues' was, true to the 'Washington consensus' developed by the IMF in close collaboration with the US Treasury, harsh deflation and measures designed further to deregulate these economies and thereby open them up to Western capital.

The most immediate effect of this was to engineer a growing socioeconomic and human catastrophe. The latest projections suggest that Indonesia's economy will contract by more than 15 percent in 1998, Thailand's by 7 or 8 percent, and South Korea's by about 5 percent.[8] In the second quarter of 1998 the Malaysian economy shrank by 6.8 percent—a huge turnaround considering that it *grew* by 7.8 percent in 1997.[9] Unemployment is soaring throughout the region, and in countries such as Indonesia the scrapping (at the IMF's insistence) of subsidies on basic commodities has caused a huge surge in the rate of inflation. Mass pauperisation, reflected in such symptoms as a huge increase in prostitution in Indonesia and Thailand, is becoming a reality. In Indonesia, John Rees writes:

> The Food and Horticulture Ministry reports that some 17 million families (or 68 million people out of a total population of 200 million) are 'hit by dire food shortages'. In central and eastern Java, the richest and most populous island in the archipelago, some 17.5 million people survive on one meal a day. Another 38 million people eat twice a day, but 'this ability is declining fast' according to the ministry.[10]

Deflation in Japan: The East Asian crisis has been exacerbated by the fact that the Japanese economy, the second biggest in the world, has stagnated throughout the present decade as a result of an earlier financial crash. The collapse of the late 1980s speculative boom centred on the stockmarkets and real estate—the so called 'bubble economy'—has left Japanese banks with huge bad loans. Standard & Poor's, the US credit ratings agency, recently estimated that problem loans in the Japanese banking system amount to 151,370 billion yen (£681 billion), a staggering 30 percent of gross domestic product.[11]

The structure of the keiretsu—the huge groups linking together industrial corporations with one of the 13 big City Banks—played the historical role of providing productive capitalists with cheap loans, but, with the banks in trouble, credit has dried up, paralysing the entire Japanese economy. To make matters worse, Japanese corporations massively invested in the rest of East Asia throughout the 1990s. Moreover, at the end of 1997 Japanese banks held claims of $191 billion on Asian emerging markets, compared to $257 billion for those of the EU and only $38 billion for US banks.[12] The regional collapse therefore deprived Japanese capitalism of badly needed profits and export markets, as well as adding a further threat to an already weakened financial system.

Japan is now caught in the same sort of deflationary spiral which gripped the world economy during the Great Depression of the 1930s. Prices are falling: in August wholesale prices were 2.1 percent lower than they were a year earlier.[13] Consumers are putting off major purchases, partly because they are afraid of rising unemployment, and partly because they expect goods to become cheaper. Starved of both domestic demand and export markets, the Japanese economy shrank throughout the first nine months of 1998, its worst performance since records began in 1955.[14] In these circumstances, conventional remedies like cutting interest rates have ceased to work. By the end of August, Japan's long term market interest rates had dropped to 1.045 percent, according to the Financial Times 'the lowest anywhere in the world for at least four centuries', and were still falling. An economist commented, 'The economic situation is now beyond gloom—it's going downhill very fast'.[15]

Faced with this very deep depression, the Bank of Japan, seizing the initiative from a paralysed government, began to show signs of a willingness to ignore the free market economic orthodoxy of the past two decades and pump money into the financial system precisely because of the inflationary consequences this might have. Many economists believe that rising prices would actually be welcome in Japan because they might stimulate more spending by consumers and companies. The difficulty with this strategy is that it would probably cause a further fall in the yen. Most East Asian currencies—with the crucial expection of the Chinese renminbi—have been massively devalued over the past year. This has made their exports cheaper, but it has also placed the Chinese economy under increasing competitive pressure.

China is suffering from many of the same problems as the rest of the region—over-capacity, bad loans and slowing growth. Intense competition has caused prices to fall steadily since October 1997. Export industries such as textiles, shipbuilding and steel have been hit hard by the devaluations elsewhere in Asia. China's exports in August 1998 were 2.4 percent lower than a year previously.[16] The vice-president of China's biggest shipmaker told the *Financial Times* that 'the yard needed a 20 percent devaluation in the Chinese currency to recoup the competitive advantage it had lost to South Korean and Japanese rivals'.[17] But a devaluation of the renminbi might spark off a further wave of competitive devaluations and financial turmoil in East Asia. So far the Beijing regime has held back from devaluation, using the threat of it to extract political favours from Washington. Nevertheless, if Tokyo were to pursue an inflationary policy, the pressure on China to devalue might become irresistible, with incalculable consequences. In October 1998 four government-backed investment companies which funnelled foreign loans to Chinese companies defaulted on their debts to international banks, raising the spectre of a financial crash in China.

The August storm: In August 1998 the financial crisis began visibly to spread from East Asia to the rest of the world. Western investors who had been willing to throw their money at emerging markets began a 'flight to quality', returning to the apparent safety of US and European financial markets. The collapse of the rouble at the end of August and Russia's effective default on its foreign loans has proved to be a decisive turning point. Market capitalism in Russia has been a hot-house plant, flourishing mainly in a few big cities, and based largely on speculative, and straightforwardly criminal, activities. Much of the foreign funds which have flowed into Russia over the past few years were immediately exported by the financial oligarchy that has flourished under Yeltsin and invested abroad. Credit Suisse First Boston estimates that in 1994-1997 capital flight from the rouble was about $66 billion. Meanwhile the economy has shrunk by 40 percent since 1991 and wage arrears amount to over a quarter of gross domestic product.[18]

What kept the Russian economy afloat was the foreign exchange earned by its exports of oil, gas, and other primary commodities. This kept the balance of payments in surplus, and thus helped to reassure foreign speculators—notably the ultra-mobile and greedy hedge funds (see below)—who bought heavily into Russian government Treasury bills, many of which, known as GKOs, had to repaid on a very short term basis (usually 30 days). This meant that large quantities of Russian government debt had to be rolled over—renewed by the sale of new GKOs—every month, making the economy highly vulnerable to the ups and downs of the financial markets.

Worries about the East Asian crisis pushed up interest rates on the GKOs to over 100 percent, while, in large part in consequence of this crisis, commodity prices fell in 1998 to their lowest levels for 20 years. As Edward Luttwak puts it:

The fall in oil and other commodity prices turned a disproportionate, and now very costly, reliance on short term debt into a financial timebomb. Foreign currency reserves kept falling, going well below the level of the monthly turnover of GKOs held by foreign investors. Everything was set for a foreign currency insolvency crisis. All that was needed was for the hedge funds to become sufficiently frightened to give up their GKOs.[19]

That's what happened in late August. The panic was precipitated, ironically enough, by a call by that arch-magician of the financial markets George Soros for the devaluation of the rouble. In previous financial crashes—for example, in Mexico in 1994-1995 and East Asia in 1997—the Group of Seven (G7) leading industrial countries and the IMF had intervened with rescue packages designed, among other things, to ensure that Western creditors got their money back. But this time the G7 stood by, perhaps partly as a way of putting pressure on Yeltsin and the Russian parliament to make sure that, whatever government, they agreed to continue with free market 'reforms'. Angry foreign banks and speculators were left holding apparently worthless Russian debt.

But the most significant economic consequence of the Russian crash has been to cause Western capital to flee other countries, particularly in Latin America and Eastern Europe. 'The shock is just so great that emerging markets will be virtually dead for a prolonged period,' said one City economist.[20] Many developing economies were already badly affected by falling prices of the primary commodities that are their main exports. Now some of them began to suffer from the same sort of capital flight that countries like South Korea had experienced in 1997. The credit ratings agency Moody's warned, 'The likelihood that countries in Latin America will resort to capital controls, debt rescheduling or debt moratoria...has increased significantly'.[21]

Brazil proved particularly vulnerable. In the first ten days of September nearly $11 billion flowed out of the country, almost as much as had left in the whole of August. The Brazilian government stemmed the outflow at least temporarily by raising interest rates to 50 percent— adding an estimated £3 billion a month to the interest payments on a budget deficit expected to reach 7-8 percent of gross domestic product, and probably precipitating the economy into recession.[22]

The Brazilian president Fernando Henrique Cardoso tried to reassure the financial markets by promising to introduce, after his re-election in early October, a crash programme of budget cuts which will almost certainly drive the economy into slump. As *The Observer* pointed out, 'The stakes are high. Brazil is the world's ninth largest economy; it accounts for 45 percent of the total gross domestic product of Latin America'.[23] A financial crash there would drag in other major regional economies such as Mexico and Argentina as well as intensifying the global panic. The consequences would be especially serious for the US. According to the *Financial Times*:

> Latin America accounts for 18 percent of US exports, against 17 percent for Asia (excluding Japan), and $20 billion of foreign direct investment against $15 billion. Around 12 percent of US companies' foreign profits come from the region, almost twice as much as from Asia's Tigers. And while European banks took the lead in lending to Russia and much of the Far East, US banks dominate south of the border. Their total cross-border exposure to Latin America, including loans, securities and derivatives, amounted to $79 billion as of March, compared with $59 billion to Asia and less than $7 billion to Russia.[24]

The crisis spreads West

US triumphalism: Until August the world economy presented a highly contradictory picture. Japan and much of the rest of Asia were in deep depression, but North America and Western Europe, accounting between them for nearly 60 percent of world output, were growing quite strongly. Wall Street continued to boom; share prices rose relentlessly, brushing off a brief downward 'correction' in October 1997, and pulling up most

Western stock exchanges.

In the US the combination of the long economic recovery since 1992 and the stockmarket boom bred a climate of euphoria in capitalist circles. Commentators argued that the so called low unemployment, low infla- tion 'Goldilocks economy' ('not too hot, not too cold') represented a 'New Economic Paradigm' that marked the end of the business cycle of boom and slump. The publisher Mortimer Zuckerman chortled in the summer of 1998:

> *The American economy is in the eighth year of sustained growth that tran-*
> *scends the 'German miracle' and the 'Japanese miracle' of earlier decades.*
> *Everything that should be up is up—GDP, capital spending, incomes, the*
> *stockmarket, employment, exports, consumer and business confidence.*
> *Everything that should be down is down—unemployment, inflation, interest*
> *rates. The United States has been ranked number one among major industrial*
> *economies for three years in a row. America is riding a capital spending*
> *boom that is modernising its industrial base and expanding its industrial*
> *capacity. The Dow Jones Industrial Average is more than four times as high*
> *as it was six years ago. The New York and NASDAQ stock exchanges have*
> *added over $4 trillion in value in the last four years alone—the largest single*
> *accumulation of wealth in the history of the United States. By contrast,*
> *Europe is stagnating and burdened with double digit unemployment, and Asia*
> *is floundering in the wake of financial collapse.*[25]

The feverish atmosphere on Wall Street encouraged even greater tri- umphalism. One money manager, James Kramer, declared, 'I believe if stocks like Bristol Myers had been around 100 years ago, there would have been no Marx, there would have been no Communism, because these stocks have made many millions of people rich'.[26] Anyone familiar with the history of capitalism will know that silly statements like these are characteristic of the peaks of speculative booms. Thus, on the eve of the great Wall Street crash of October 1929, the financier John J Raskob, in an article called 'Everybody Ought to be Rich', came out with a plan to allow the poor to make money on the stockmarket. The appearance of such nonsense may indeed be a sign that a crash is on the way. Such, at any rate, proved to be the case both in 1929 and in 1998.

A common US response to the Asian crisis was nevertheless to greet it with indifference or even to gloat. Many commentators claimed it marked the triumph of free market Anglo-American capitalism over its more regulated and interventionist rivals. The financial crash was explained away as a consequence of Asian 'crony capitalism': the proper workings of the market had been undermined by interfering bureaucrats bribed by firms which benefited from government protection. The Asian 'miracle'—only a couple of years before hailed as the future of world capitalism—was now forgotten. 'Korea is one of the last transitional economies to market capitalism,' the economist David Hale patronisingly explained, comparing it, quite absurdly, with East Germany.[27]

From this perspective, the East Asian collapse could even be welcomed as an opportunity for Western capital further to penetrate and profitably to restructure economies which usually had hitherto been dominated by local firms enjoying close relations with the state bureaucracy. The *Financial Times* reported in the spring of 1998 that 'East Asia's demand for fresh capital to clear up loans is providing Western institutions with unprecedented leverage. The conditions attached to International Monetary Fund and World Bank rescue programmes are playing a role in prising open Asia's closed corporate cultures, creating opportunities for international companies.' Adlai Stevenson, US senator turned investment banker, gloated, 'The opportunity for investment, whether in production, distribution or portfolio assets, is once in a lifetime'.[28]

Alan Greenspan, chairman of the US central bank, the Federal Reserve Board, summed up this triumphalist mood: 'My sense is that one consequence of this Asian crisis is an increasing awareness in the region that market capitalism, as practised in the West, especially in the US, is the superior model; that is, it provides greater promise of producing rising standards of living and continuous growth'.[29] As recently as June 1998 he speculated that the US economy might have moved 'beyond history'—beyond, that is, the cycle of boom and slump and onto an endless upward path.

Underlying problems: The August crisis soon made Greenspan sing a different tune: 'It is not credible that the US can remain an oasis of prosperity unaffected by a world that is experiencing greatly increased stress,' he admitted.[30] Following the Russian collapse, Wall Street and the other major stockmarkets fell sharply at the end of August. 'What we are witnessing now in terms of the breadth and depth of value diminution is the biggest collapse in security markets since the war,' said one investment banker.[31] As one Wall Street stockbroker put it, 'We have seen the upside of globalisation for the last seven years; now we are seeing the downside'.[32]

Despite brief upward blips, share prices carried on falling. The 'flight to quality' increasingly took investors away from the stockmarkets and into the interest-bearing bonds issued by governments. In consequence real yields on government bonds in the advanced capitalist world fell significantly below the average for the previous 20 years. This shift in mood reflected more than the fear that Asian 'contagion' was now beginning to affect Western financial markets.

The 'New Economic Paradigm' hailed by light-minded capitalist apologists in the US rested on very weak foundations. Joel Geier and Ahmed Shawki pointed out:

> *This much celebrated economic expansion, though long, is weak both in terms of growth and productivity as compared to previous post World War II booms... After six years of expansion the economy had grown by 31.5 percent in the 1960s (5.25 percent a year), by 24.2 percent in the 1980s (4.0 percent a year), and in the 1990s by 15.5 percent (2.6 percent). The expansion of the 1970s only lasted for four and a half years so comparisons are more difficult. In that expansion there was growth of 15.5 percent in the first three years, while it has taken six years for the expansion of the 1990s to produce similar results.*[33]

US gross domestic product did grow by nearly 4 percent in 1997, but this is more likely to be seen as the Indian summer of the 1990s recovery than a breakthrough to an era of unlimited expansion. Claims made by boosters for an unparalled revolution in US productivity also do no stand up to close examination.[34] They are best understood as ways of justifying and sustaining the continuing rise of shares on the stockmarket than as descriptions of economic reality.

This boom in fact depended on massive borrowing by both companies and households. The unorthodox economist Wynne Godley pointed out that the US private sector's financial surplus—the excess of income over expenditure—had fallen from its average since 1953 of 1.1 percent of gross domestic product to a record deficit of 3.3 percent in the first quarter of 1998. This excess of spending over income was being financed by borrowing that was growing at an unsustainable rate:

> *As the private sector's deficit is now at a level where large injections of finance are needed just to maintain it where it is, it can hardly go on growing much longer. For this deficit to go on growing, the ratio of debt to income, which is already rising fast, would have to accelerate out of sight.*
>
> *This means that the motor which has driven the US economy through one 'Goldilocks era'—namely the expansion of private spending financed by loans— cannot possibly drive it through another. It looks more as though it is ready to conk out.*[35]

By the time this diagnosis appeared in July 1998, concern about the future course of the US economy was growing. Greenspan warned that he might have to increase interest rates to prevent a revival in inflation caused, in all probability, by the comparatively low rate of unemployment—4.5 percent in June. Workers might, in other words, use the greater bargaining power provided by tight labour markets to push up wages. Meanwhile, the US economy was showing definite signs of slowing down as companies' inventories of finished goods increased sharply.

The logic of financial panic: The biggest economy in the world was thus already facing difficulties even before the August crisis. What would be the latter's impact on North America and Western Europe? Economists and brokers referred to the danger of 'contagion', as if the growing panic were some sinister and incomprehensible disease. In fact, the spreading crisis was promoted by many of the same features of financial markets— their capacity to move capital very quickly across national borders, and the variety of avenues they offer for speculation—that have been celebrated by the boosters of globalisation over the past decade.

Financial crises have a tendency to feed off themselves. Will Hutton describes the dynamics of this process:

> *It is when the flows of credit and capital within and between countries get undermined by the incapacity of banks to continue underwriting these flows, because their balance sheets become so weakened, that downturns become slumps. A vicious circle is created in which the combination of actual losses and collapsing confidence causes financiers to cut back their readiness to lend and invest, which in turn means that output, employment and demand fall, which in turn generates more financial losses.*[36]

The process is the reverse of what generates the financial boom in the first place. Charles Kindleberger argues that a speculative mania is characterised by what the classical economists call 'overtrading':

> *It may involve pure speculation for a price rise, an overestimate of prospective returns, or excessive 'gearing'. Pure speculation, of course, involves buying for resale rather than use in the case of commodities, or for resale rather income in the case of financial assets. Overestimation of profits comes from euphoria, [and] affects firms engaged in the productive and distributive processes... Excessive gearing arises from cash requirements which are low relative both to the prevailing price of a good or asset and to possible changes.*[37]

Margin trading is a classic example of excessive gearing (or leverage, as it is often also called). Investors buy stocks (or other financial assets) by advancing only a fraction of the purchase price and borrowing the rest from a bank or a stockbroker, with the stock itself as collateral. The speculator hopes the price of the stock will rise sufficiently that by the time repayment of the loan falls due he or she can come away with a profit. This is a perfect device for those gambling on prices continuing to rise, since they only have to put a relatively small amount of cash upfront. But what happens if the price falls below what it cost to buy it? Then the bank or broker demands more cash to make up the collateral on the loan. If share prices are falling generally, a vicious circle develops in which these margin calls force investors to sell up to find the cash, causing prices to fall further, and thus producing yet more margin calls, and so on. This process was central to the great Wall Street crash of October 1929.[38]

Some experts think that this may be happening again. Ignoring the history of past financial crashes, much speculation is highly geared. The global hedge funds play a crucial role here. These have developed over the last decade, and operate unregulated by any national government. They make their profits by gambling on the ways in which the differences between the prices of various financial assets are likely to change over time. Hedge funds are estimated to have between them some $400 billion, and often borrow five or six times this amount—sometimes, as we shall see below, far, far more.[39] David Zervos of Greenwich NatWest estimates that there are about $60,000 billion worth of financial assets involved in margin trading and similar kinds of leverage. If, as is quite plausible, the value of these assets were to fall by $1,500 billion, the banks might start making margin calls. 'If there was a failure of one or large counterparties to meet the margin call, the resulting sale of collateral and liquidation of swap positions could easily drive spreads further and induce even more widening, more margin calls, and a complete collapse in the credit market'.[40]

Some hint of the potential dangers came in late September when the Federal Reserve Board co-ordinated a $3.5 billion bailout by a consortium of 15 major American and European investment banks of Long Term Capital Management, one of the largest US hedge funds. LTCM had made very healthy profits for its investors by using highly elaborate mathematical models to guide its bets that the differences between the prices of various bonds would narrow. Its boss, John Meriwether, was a legendary figure on Wall Street from his time as head of Salomon Brothers' bond trading operations during the Reagan boom in the 1980s. His staff included two Nobel prize winning economists and a former vice-chairman of the Fed, David Mullins. Success encouraged very high gearing—LTCM's capital of $4.8 billion supported at the peak an incredible $900 billion of market exposure.[41]

Then came the August crisis. The flight to quality caused the differences between bond prices to widen spectacularly as investors fled to the safety of US and German government bonds. LTCM started taking huge losses that were exacerbated by a series of margin calls. Its capital was soon wiped out. When Barings faced a similar crisis in February 1995 thanks to Nick Leeson's catastrophic derivatives trading it was allowed to go bust. But this time the threat was far more serious. 'Many of the banks realised that if we went through a forced unwind of our derivatives positions, they might be taken down with us,' said a source in the hedge fund.[42]

It turned out there were all kinds of cosy links between LTCM and its rescuers. David Mullins had, while working at the Fed, investigated a bond rigging scandal which led to Meriwether's resignation from Salomon in 1991. He remained a friend of Greenspan, who directed the rescue. David Kosminsky, chairman of Merrill Lynch, one of the banks that took over LTCM, had invested in the fund. So had the Bank of Italy, and UBS, Europe's biggest bank, whose chairman was forced to resign over the resulting loss of £413 million. The affair revealed what the financial journalist John Plender called 'Western crony capitalism'.[43]

Towards financial armageddon? More important than the corruption and incompetence it revealed, the LTCM collapse suggested that the financial markets were becoming caught in a vicious downward spiral. The end-game of the kind of financial crisis we are now experiencing is a credit crunch. During a speculative boom all sorts of credit are easy to come by. When a panic ensues, however, investors rush for safety into the most secure forms of money—gold in the past, now the currencies and government bonds of the strongest economies. At the climax of this process, they refuse to risk their money in any sort of investment, and seek cash as the ultimate security. Other assets are desperately sold in order to obtain it, even if this forces down prices.

This process can be reinforced when government policy is ruled by *laissez faire* orthodoxy which relies on the unregulated market to restore equilibrium. Thus Andrew Mellon, US Treasury Secretary during the onset of the Great Depression at the end of the 1920s, declared that the solution of the crisis was to 'liquidate labour, liquidate stocks, liquidate the farmers, liquidate real estate'.[44] In fact, as Keynes pointed out at the time, this remedy only makes matters worse. The falling prices and rising unemployment caused by the forced sale of assets reduce the income of both workers and capitalists and thereby cuts the demand for goods and services. The resulting bankruptcies and layoffs initiate yet another twist to the downward spiral.

Long before Keynes, Marx had outlined the irrational logic of this process, in which money is preferred to the commodities whose value it embodies:

In times of a squeeze, when credit contracts or ceases entirely, money sud-denly stands as the only means of payment and true existence of value in absolute opposition to all other commodities. Hence the universal deprecia-tion of commodities, the difficulty or even impossibility of transforming them into money, ie into their own purely fantastic form. Secondly, however, credit money itself is only money to the extent that it absolutely takes the place of actual money to the amount of its nominal amount value... Hence coercive measures, raising the rate of interest etc, for the purpose of safeguarding the conditions of this convertibility... A depreciation of credit-money...would unsettle all existing relations. Therefore, the value of commodities is sacri-ficed for the purpose of safeguarding the fantastic and indepependent existence of this value in money. As money-value, it is only secure as long as money is secure. For a few millions in money, many millions in commodities must be sacrificed. This is inevitable under capitalist production and consti-tutes one of its beauties... As long as the social character of labour appears as the money-existence of commodities, and thus as a thing external to actual production, money crises— independent of or as an intensification of actual crises—are inevitable. [45]

Precisely this kind of process is now at work in Western financial markets. Falling share and bond prices were tearing huge chunks off the value of investments: the Federal Reserve estimates that the net loss of wealth in US financial assets between July and October 1998 amounted to $1,500 billion.[46] Increasingly, investors shunned the shares and bonds of even the biggest private corporations. The share prices of many of the major investment and commercial banks, seen as major victims of the financial crises, halved between mid-August and early October, and their credit ratings were being slashed. The *Financial Times* reported:

The 'flight to quality', in other words, is turning into a flight from quality, and into AAA-rated havens—US Treasury bonds and German government bonds... Broadly speaking, liquidity—the ease with which an investor can buy or sell a security—has dried up in all but the safest government bond markets... 'Investors normally look for a return on their capital,' said Avinash Persaud, head of currency research at JP Morgan. 'Now all they are doing is trying to preserve its value: capital retention as opposed to capital enhancement'. [47]

One effect of the credit crunch was to increase the interest payments companies have to make on their bonds in order to attract investors. The *Financial Times* commented, 'The longer this continues the more likely it is that companies will default on their existing debt, as they will be unable to refinance it through the bond markets. Higher defaults would lead to higher unemployment and lower growth'.[48] The same mechanisms are at work in the currency markets. In early October the dollar fell sharply against the yen. Japanese financial institutions, loaded down with bad debts and therefore short of cash, sold dollars heavily. So did the hedge funds. Before the August crisis they had taken advantage of the weakness of the yen and the low level of Japanese interest rates to borrow cheap in Japan and use the money to invest in apparently more profitable assets elsewhere—for example, Russian government bonds. Now this 'yen carry trade' was turning against the hedge funds, as their losses forced them to sell the dollar and buy yen to repay their debts. The fear this raised of yet more collapses such as that of LTCM encouraged investors to hang onto their money, making liquidity even more scarce. Even US government bonds were dumped as investors sought the ulti-mate safe haven of cash itself.

Trade Wars? Currency volatility is in any case a further destabilising factor. Most East Asian countries' currencies fell massively against other currencies during the financial crash of the second half of 1997. As a result, their exports have become much more competitive. Moreover, Asian firms and governments have a powerful incentive to export in order to restore profitability and repay foreign loans. About a third of US foreign trade and 10 percent of the EU's is with Japan and the rest of East Asia. US and European firms are having to compete with cheaper exports from Asia at the same time the region's economy—and therefore its demand for imports—is shrinking.[49] The Institute for International Economics estimates that the Asian crisis will reduce Western Europe's net exports by $55 billion a year and the US's by $43 billion.[50]

The massive US balance of payments deficit during the 1980s and early 1990s caused major conflicts over trade between the three major capitalist trading blocs—the US, Japan, and Western Europe. Similar ten-sions are already beginning to develop. The US steel industry charged its Japanese counterpart with dumping after Japanese steel exports to the US rose in August 1998 to 3.6 times their level a year previously. Japanese steelmakers, faced with a depressed domestic economy and the collapse of their main Asian markets, had redirected their exports towards the US and Taiwan.[51] European steel producers are also lobbying Brussels for anti-dumping measures against Asian importers. Meanwhile, the rise in continental European currencies (and soon the euro) against the dollar could accelerate the developing economic slowdown in the EU. Since 1995 continental Europe has benefited from the strength of the dollar, and the consequent relative cheapness of its exports, but if the US currency's fall is sustained, this competitive advantage will disappear.

The rate of profit

Financial crises and productive capital: The most visible form of the crisis so far has been the spreading financial panic. In its face, Alan Greenspan, long regarded by leading capitalists as possessing positively magical powers, confessed bewilderment. He told a conference of economists that he had never seen anything like the events in financial markets since August. But he denied that the market was the problem: 'A major shift towards liquidity protection is really not a market phenomenon. It's a fear-induced psychological reaction'.[52]

In fact, as we have seen, developments over the past few months fit into a very familiar pattern characteristic of financial crises under capitalism. There is now a growing chorus of criticism of the prevailing free market orthodoxy, mainly from a Keynesian or social democratic point of view which does not reject capitalism as such but argues that markets need to be regulated. Such critics generally highlight the inherent instability of financial markets. Thus George Soros (who knows a thing or two about financial markets) wrote after the Asian financial crash:

> *The private sector is ill-suited to allocate international credit. It provides either too little or too much. It does not have the information with which to form a balanced judgement. Moreover, it is not concerned with maintaining macro-economic balance in the borrowing countries. Its goals are to maximise profit and minimise risk. This makes it move in a herd-like fashion in both directions.*
>
> *The excess always begins with overexpansion, and the correction is always associated with pain. But with the intervention of the IMF and other official lenders, the pain is felt more by the borrowers more than by the creditors. That is why overexpansion has occurred so often after each crisis. Successive crises have, however, become more difficult to handle.*[53]

This analysis is important because it underlines that the East Asian crisis was not a product of local 'crony capitalism'. Highly mobile speculative investment from the advanced countries first raised up the Tiger economies and then brought them crashing down. Soros's diagnosis recalls Keynes's famous analysis of the irrationality of financial markets: 'Speculators may do no harm as bubbles on a steady stream of enterprise. But the position is serious when enterprise becomes the bubble of a whirlwind of speculation. When the capital development of a country becomes the byproduct of a casino, the job is likely to be ill-done'.[54]

Social democratic economists such as Will Hutton of *The Observer* and Larry Elliott of *The Guardian* have in recent years revived the Keynesian critique of financial markets.[55] The other side of this critique is, however, the argument that, provided the excesses of speculation are curbed and the market properly regulated, capitalism can avoid serious slumps. By comparison with that offered by the Marxist tradition, this is a relatively superficial theory of crisis which fails to locate the sources of the cycle of boom and slump in the dynamics of the capitalist mode of production itself.[56]

Thus Marx distinguishes between productive capital and money-capital. The former is invested in the employment of wage labourers who produce commodities and in the process have surplus value extracted from them. Money-capitalists—bankers, for example, and shareholders—perform the function of advancing capital for productive investment; their profits derive ultimately from a portion of the surplus value that is created elsewhere, in the process of production. The various kinds of asset traded on financial markets—shares, bonds, derivatives, and the like—are thus 'fictitious capital', since they constitute, not actual investments in the production of commodities and extraction of surplus value, but rather claims on that surplus value:

> The stocks of railways, mines, navigation companies, and the like, represent actual capital, namely the capital invested and functioning in such enterprises, or the amount of money advanced by stockholders for the purpose of being used as capital in such enterprises... But this capital does not exist twice, once as the capital-value of titles of ownership (stocks) on the one hand and on the other hand as the actual capital invested, or to be invested, in those enterprises. It exists only in the latter form, and a share of stock is merely a title of ownership to a corresponding portion of the surplus value to be realized.[57]

Productive capitalists may use financial markets as a way of raising money for their investments. But the assets created in the process, like money-capital in general, represent 'an accumulation of claims of ownership upon labour'.[58] At the same time, however, these assets gain a life of their own on the financial markets by becoming objects of speculation. Back at the dawn of modern capitalism in the 17th century, the Dutch called financial speculation *windhandel*—'trading in wind'.[59] Even tulips became the object of frenzied buying during the mania of 1636-1637.[60] In contemporary derivatives markets, assets such as the option to buy some other asset for a given price at some point in future are traded on the basis of values that are ultimately derived from, say, the price of a commodity or an exchange rate.

Rudolf Hilferding provided the classic Marxist account of speculation:

> Speculative gains or losses arise only from variations in the current valuations of claims to interest. They are neither profit, nor parts of surplus value,

*but originate in fluctuations in the valuations of that part of surplus value
which the corporation assigns to the shareholders... They are purely marginal gains. Whereas the capitalist class as a whole appropriates a part of the
labour of the proletariat without giving anything in return, speculators gain
only from each other. One's loss is the other's gain. 'Les affairs, c'est
l'argent des autres.'* [Business is other people's money][61]

Speculators, in other words, make their profits by correctly antici-
pating the direction in which the prices of particular assets, or the
differences between them, change. As in more everyday kinds of gambling, the losses of those who get their bets wrong provide the successful
speculators with their profits. But the movements of the financial
markets are ultimately regulated by those of productive capital.
Speculators' profits may derive from changes in the prices of financial
assets, but these prices in turn depend on expectations about the profits
generated in production. When the stockmarket develops ahead of productive capital for too long, a crash is inevitable.

In October 1997 the value of US stocks was 130 percent of what it
would cost to replace the net assets of companies. 'This is higher than at
any time since 1920, double its long-run average and about three times
higher than a decade ago,' the free market economist Martin Wolf commented. He suggested the stockmarket was moving way out of line of the
real economy:

*Combined with economic growth running at around 3 percent, the recovery in
the share of profits in GDP has generated growth in profits of 10 percent a
year in real terms since 1992. This recovery has underpinned the stockmarket
surge. Yet for anything like this to continue over the next five years, the share
of GDP in profits must reach unprecedented levels.*[62]

Towards a crisis of profitability? The behaviour of profits is thus a critical determinant of the future course of the crisis. The underlying
profitability of capital accordingly constitutes the second dimension of
our analysis. Marx argued that the main driving force behind capitalist
crises lies in what he called the tendency of the rate of profit to fall.
Competition forces capitalists to expand their investments in plant and
equipment more quickly than the workers they employ. The organic
composition of capital—the ratio between capital invested in means of
production and capital invested in labour power—rises. But, since it is
workers who create the surplus value that is the source of profits, this
means that profits will grow more slowly than total investment. In other
words, the rate of profit—the return the capitalists make on the capital
they have advanced—falls. When the rate of profit falls sufficiently low
to discourage capitalists from making further investments, an economic

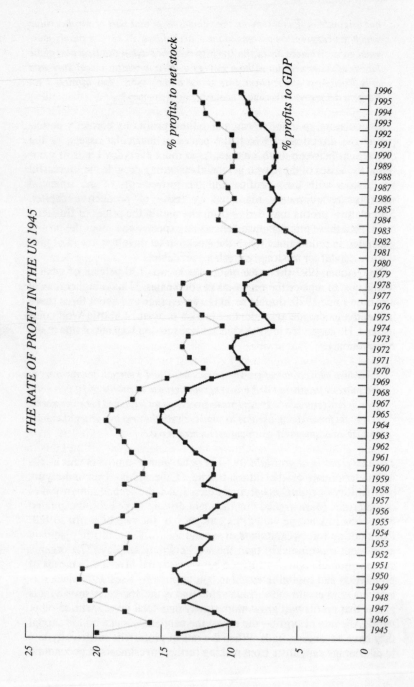

crisis is inevitable.[63]

It was a pronounced fall in the rate of profit in all the major capitalist economies during the late 1960s and early 1970s which ushered the present prolonged period of economic instability and stagnation. In their major attempt to apply Marxist value-theory to the US economy in a theoretically and empirically rigorous way, Anwar Shaikh and Ahmet Tonak show that the value-composition of fixed capital (a relationship closely connected with the organic composition of capital) rose by over 77 percent between 1948 and 1980, with the biggest rise taking place in the mid-1970s, and the rate of profit falling by a third. As they say, 'This is striking empirical support for Marx's theory of the falling rate of profit'.[64]

Shin Gyoung-hee has demonstrated that a crisis of profitability in South Korean manufacturing industry underlay last year's financial crash.[65] What about the advanced capitalist countries? There have been a number of claims recently that the biggest economy of all, the United States, has finally restored the rate of profit to levels last seen during the long postwar boom. The *Financial Times* reported last summer, 'Profit margins, lifted by the long economic expansion and tight control on labour costs have...risen to levels last seen in the 1960s'.[66] Even Robert Brenner, in a major attempt at a Marxist analysis of postwar capitalism, seemed to agree: 'Despite the weakness of the cyclical upturn, the rate of profit in the private business sector has increased steadily in the course of the 1990s. By 1996 it had, for the first time, decisively surpassed its level of 1973, achieving its level of 1969, 20-25 percent below its boom time peaks. By 1997 it had come back even further'.[67]

These claims are not supported by a study of the the rate of profit in the US by the Bureau of Economic Statistics, using Department of Commerce data (see graph).[68] If we compare profits with net stock (plant, equipment, and machinery net of depreciation) we find that the rate of profit in 1996 was 9.38 percent, about the same as it was in 1971 (9.44 percent), a pretty bad year for the US economy by the standards of the long boom. Joel Geier and Ahmed Shawki summarise the overall results of the study:

In the post-war boom years, 1946-1968, corporate profits to corporate net stock ranged from 11-15 percent, except for two recession years. In the run up to crisis from 1969-1973, the rate of profit fell from 13 percent to between 8.8 and 11 percent. Since 1973, the rate of profit averaged 7.3 percent and ranged from 4.7 to 9 percent. In 1996 it rose to 9.4 percent, higher than any year since 1973. Although better than the recovery years of the 1980s, it is very similar to the profit rates of the first crisis recovery in 1976-1978. These rates cannot be compared to the post-war boom; they are not even as good as the recession years of the 1940s, 1950s or 1960s.[69]

This performance in the US needs to be set again the background of a sustained and brutal employers' offensive since the mid-1970s—20 years of falling real wages, deregulation, downsizing, and soaring corporate profits and executive salaries. Brenner summarises the price the US working class paid so that profits could recover from the depths they fell to in the early 1980s:

*Between 1979 and 1990, real hourly compensation in the private business economy grew at an average annual rate of 0.1 percent. The trend in these years was for hourly real wages and salaries alone (excluding benefits) was far worse, **falling** at an average amount of 1 percent. At no time previously in the 20th century had real wage growth been anywhere near so low for anywhere near so long.*[70]

But despite this increase in the rate of exploitation of labour, the US ruling class has still been unable to push the rate of profit above the levels to which it had fallen on the eve of the first great post-war slump in the mid-1970s. And it is likely to be downhill from here. Corporate profits in the US have been falling since the last quarter of 1997. They are being squeezed from two directions. Intensified competition from cheap Asian exports will make it harder for US capitalists to raise prices. Meanwhile the lowest rate of unemployment in a generation has allowed workers finally to push up real wages, which have risen since at an annual rate of 2.6 percent since 1996.[71]

The same pressures are beginning to make themselves felt in the EU as well. The rash of plant closures in Britain by both local and multinational firms reflect both the specific problem caused by the strength of the pound, which has made British exports relatively expensive, and the more general impact of the competitive struggle to find markets. The British economy is out of phase with that of the rest of Europe, most of which has only begun to grow strongly since the mid-1990s, while Britain is plainly heading rapidly for a recession. But the global slowdown is beginning to affect continental Europe as well, as projections for company profits and growth rates are slashed.

The crisis of policy

Warnings of doom: There is, then, little doubt that world capitalism is heading towards its fourth major recession since the early 1970s. How serious will the slump be? Some influential economic commentators have begun to warn of the danger of a depression on the scale of the 1930s. Will Hutton declared, 'The risk of a world economic catastrophe may be slight, but it is growing by the day'.[72] 'What is now at stake', he claimed, 'is nothing less than the viability of the world financial and trade order put in place over the last 20 years'.[73] On the free market right, Martin Wolf of the *Financial Times* put forward a remarkably similar prognosis: 'What is happening in the "emerging market" economies is a disaster... The question is whether it will become a worldwide catastrophe. The chances may be small. They are not, alas, zero'.[74]

A critical factor in determining the development of the crisis is the response of the major capitalist states. During the present period of crises which began in the late 1960s, state intervention has not been able to prevent recessions or remove their underlying causes, but it has been sufficient to stave off a slump on the scale of the 1930s. Therefore the third dimension of the crisis that needs to be considered is government policy.

The reaction against the free market: Over the past 20 years free market economics has become entrenched as unchallengeable orthodoxy in the Western ruling classes. Though the vanguard of the 'New Right', represented by Reagan and Thatcher, has been pushed out of office in most places, the 1990s has seen the emergence of a 'centre-left' strongly committed to Thatcherite economics. Thus Bill Clinton accepted the Republican right's agenda of deficit cutting and welfare 'reform'. Tony Blair and Gordon Brown have been faithful pupils of Clinton. Their first, and most significant, policy measure was to give the Bank of England control over interest rates. Brown wrote a Thatcherite commitment to reduce public spending and abstain from economic intervention into his Code of Fiscal Stability.

The idea of independent central banks has become one of the main planks of monetarist dogma. It is intended to help insulate the market from any sort of democratic political control and leave the economy on autopilot. European Economic and Monetary Union, due to take full effect with the launch of the single currency at the beginning of 1999, will vest control over monetary policy into a European Central Bank (ECB) guided by a particularly narrow version of monetarism. The ECB's remit, like that of the Bank of England, is solely to achieve price stability, making it difficult for it to play the traditional role of central banks as 'lender of last resort', pumping money into the financial system where it is threatened with complete collapse.[75] Meanwhile, the targets laid down by the Maastricht treaty, that participating governments must reduce their budget deficits to no more than 3 percent of national income, will continue to operate, under the EU's Growth and Stability Pact, throughout the euro-zone.[76]

The major Western governments thus face the developing economic crisis with the same kind of rigid free market policies which helped push the world economy into the Great Depression of the 1930s. But a powerful reaction to these policies is beginning to set in. Thus various free market economists, notably Jeffrey Sachs, architect of the disastrous programme of 'shock therapy' forced through in Russia and Eastern Europe in the early 1990s, attacked the IMF for the harsh deflationary measures it demanded of South Korea and the other Tiger economies in exchange for lending them enough money to keep afloat (and repay their Western creditors). According to Sachs:

> ...the IMF has decided to impose a severe macroeconomic contraction on top of the market panic that is already roiling [sic] these economies. Consider the Korea programme... The Fund argues that these draconian monetary measures are 'to restore and sustain calm in the markets' and '[to] demonstrate the government's resolve to confront the present crisis'. It is hard to see how recessionary monetary measures will restore calm. Indeed the panic has so intensified since the signing of the agreement that Korean banks may now be on the verge of outright default.[77]

Faced with economic collapse, governments have in fact been forced to violate free market dogma. In October 1997 the South Korean government nationalised the bankrupt car maker Kia. More serious still have been the challenges to the free movement of capital, one of the IMF's most beloved dogmas. During the financial turmoil caused by the August 1998 crisis, Malaysian prime minister Mahathir Mohamad imposed strict exchange controls, and sacked his deputy, Anwar Ibrahim. As finance minister, Anwar had imposed a severe squeeze on the Malaysian economy. Mahathir now told banks to lend freely to industrial companies in order to keep them afloat. 'The free market system has failed and failed disastrously,' he said. 'The only way that we can manage the economy is to insulate us...from speculators'.[78]

Even more remarkable, in that island of free market capitalism, Hong Kong, the Monetary Authority intervened vigorously in the stockmarket, buying $14 billion worth of shares in order to push up prices and prevent its currency from being forced off its peg to the US dollar. The Taiwanese government announced it was reviewing plans to scrap all capital controls by the end of 2000. Shea Jia-dong, deputy governor of Taiwan's central bank, said, 'When we established the goal, there was no such thing as Asia's financial crisis, but in the light of that crisis we have to consider whether to move to completely free capital flows'.[79]

In Russia, even the *Financial Times*'s ultra-orthodox Lex column admitted that 'the only alternative [to the collapse of the rouble] is to slam on exchange controls'.[80] The appointment of Yevgeny Primakov, a veteran of the Soviet era, as prime minister in mid-September represented a shift towards a more regulated economy. In an earlier speech he

had criticised Russian governments for sacrificing economic growth to
the financial stability demanded by the IMF and called for a Roosevelt-
style New Deal.[81] 'An anti-market backlash has begun,' the *Financial
Times* announced:

> *Policy makers and economists are increasingly questioning whether or not it
> is appropriate to impose a single model of Anglo-Saxon capitalism in coun-
> tries at very different stages of development. Debate is focusing in particular
> on whether countries should allow investment capital to flow unimpeded
> across their borders, as the International Monetary Fund suggests they
> should.*[82]

Political paralysis: The Keynesian commentator William Keegan wrote
recently, 'It is difficult to take the scale of the defeat suffered by the
people responsible for the economic policy consensus of recent years'.[83]
This shift in attitudes—even the IMF itself grudgingly conceded that the
free movement of capital could have damaging consequences[84]—
prompted another leading Keynesian, *The Guardian*'s Larry Elliott, to
say that 'the debate now is about the form intervention should take,
rather than whether it should happen'.[85]

Initiatives by the G7 did manage to stave off financial collapse in the
recent past. When Mexico defaulted on its foreign debt in August 1982,
threatening the survival of the US banks that had lent heavily to Latin
America, the Fed slashed interest rates. After Black Monday, the stockmarket crash of 19 October 1987, Greenspan led the other Western
central banks in an operation designed to stabilise the world economy by
cutting interest rates and pumping money into the financial system.[86]
When Mexico experienced another financial crash in 1994-1995, Clinton
co-ordinated a massive rescue programme by the G7 and the IMF.

The US did in fact intervene fairly vigorously in the early stages of
the present crisis, after the Asian financial crash. In the autumn of 1997,
Washington acted to block proposals backed by the Japanese government for a special Asian fund to co-ordinate the rescue of the Tiger
economies. By ensuring that it was the IMF which signed agreements
with Thailand, South Korea and Indonesia, the Clinton administration
ensured that the conditions imposed would require market 'reforms'
designed to open the Asian economies further up to Western investment.
As IMF managing director Michel Camdessus put it, 'What we are doing
coincides with the basic purposes of American diplomacy in the world'.[87]

When the IMF agreement with South Korea looked like collapsing
just before Christmas 1997, the US Treasury Secretary, Robert Rubin,
initiated discussions leading to a $10 billion emergency loan to Seoul in
exchange for tough conditions, notably labour 'reforms' making it easier

for employers to sack workers and vary wages. Central bankers held meetings with the bosses of the big commercial banks in the G7 countries in order to persuade them to start rolling over their loans to South Korea.[88] Yet, faced with an escalating crisis in the autumn of 1998, the leaders of the major capitalist economies offered nothing but words. No rescue was mounted for Russia, while the only immediate measures taken were tiny cuts in US, British and Canadian interest rates. At the end of the IMF's and World Bank's annual meetings in Washington, the Indian finance minister, Yashwant Sinha, expressed his frustration: 'The brute fact is that after five days of intense discussion and debate, we are still at a loss to explain why contagion has continued to spread. Nor do we seem to have clear, agreed and effective measures to contain the crisis'.[89]

This pathetic response reflected, in the first place, a vacuum of political leadership in the bourgeois world. Bill Clinton declared that the world economy was facing its most serious challenge for 50 years, and affirmed, 'America can and must continue to act and to lead'.[90] But he had his mind on other things, and, in his greatly weakened position, was unable to secure from Congress such key requirements of US foreign policy as renewed 'fast-track' authority to negotiate more pacts like the North American Free Trade Agreement. Meanwhile, Germany was distracted by the federal elections and the formation of a new government, and the Liberal Democrat regime in Japan seemed totally paralysed in the face of the country's slump.

The failure to act was, secondly, a consequence of the fact that the cycles of the three major Western economies were out of synchronisation. Japanese interest rates were already the lowest in the history of capitalism. After stagnating for much of the present decade, the continental European economy began to grow again in the late 1990s. The European Commission estimated that the euro-zone was growing at an annual rate of 3 percent in the spring of 1998. Although this recovery was not strong enough to reduce German unemployment below 4 million, it was sufficient to worry the notoriously conservative Bundesbank about a revival in inflation.

Its chiefs bitterly remember how the reaction to the 1987 crash helped to stoke up inflation in the US, Japan, and Britain, and thus to precipitate the recession of the early 1990s. They also resent that EU countries paid the lion's share of the 1995 Mexican rescue, thus protecting the US speculators who had poured money into Mexico from suffering for their mistakes. The Bundesbank is obsessed with the 'moral hazard' which arises when economic actors are allowed to escape the consequences of their actions. While as we have seen, some free market economists have attacked the IMF for imposing deflationary policies on crisis-hit economies, German central bankers believe that IMF rescue plans have been too lax, in particular by encouraging speculators to undertake risky investments confident that they would be bailed out if things went wrong. According to Wolfgang Munchau:

> *Hans Tietmeyer, president of the Bundesbank, hardly misses an opportunity these days to warn about moral hazard and to call for economic reform in the affected countries as a necessary condition to a solution... At a recent conference in Frankfurt, organised jointly by the Bundesbank and the IMF, senior German officials publicly berated the IMF's top management. Jürgen Stark, then a senior German finance ministry official and now vice-president of the Bundesbank, argued that the IMF's bailout of Mexico after the 1994 crisis had directly contributed to the current crisis... Taken a step further, his reasoning suggests that the IMF not only failed to prevent the current crisis, it actually caused it by lulling investors into a false sense of security... It is an unfortunate fact that some sections of the German financial establishment look on the IMF as a gang of economic terrorists.*[91]

The European Central Bank, which will take control of monetary policy in the euro-zone on 1 January 1999, is likely to pursue similarly conservative policies in order to prove to financial markets that it is as tough on inflation as the Bundesbank. Wim Duisenberg, the ECB president, dismissed talk of crisis as 'overdone', and denied that there was any need for action. 'We will see about a crisis if that event arrives,' he said.[92] This complacency is strikingly reminiscent of central bankers' response to the onset of the Great Depression of the 1930s.

But, thirdly, the political paralysis reflects the sheer intractability of the crisis. Many of the remedies canvassed are simply an irrelevance. The introduction of capital controls has become, as we have seen, a popular remedy. Chile's tax on short term inflows of capital is frequently cited as a model, for example by sociologist Anthony Giddens, theoretician of the Blairite 'third way'.[93] No one seemed to notice that, since the Asian crash, Chile, like other 'emerging markets', has been suffering from a huge *outflow* of capital. As a result, the central bank been forced to push up overnight interest rates to as high as 100 percent on occasion, the Chilean peso has been devalued, and the economy is slowing down fast.[94]

More radical remedies include the Tobin Tax on financial speculation, and the reform of the international monetary system. Most versions of the latter are little more than platitudes, like Blair's call in a speech to the New York stock exchange for greater 'transparency' from the IMF.[95] Will Hutton argues more robustly that 'establishing a world central bank is the obvious next step'.[96] Like the Tobin Tax, this measure would require the existence of a global authority with the capacity to coerce national capitalist classes with their divergent, and often conflicting interests—a world state, in other words. It is the purest kind of reformist Utopia.

Others such as Larry Elliott advocate measures comparable to the Marshall Plan which revived West European capitalism after the Second World War. Thus G7 could fend off slump by pumping capital into the world economy. But the Marshall Plan was introduced in the context of a rapidly expanding capitalist system benefiting from the high levels of profitability made possible by the permanent arms economy. Moreover, the US ruling class was agreed that revitalising the European economy was essential to counter Russia in the Cold War. But no such agreement exists now. After the rescues of the past few years, the IMF has only $10 billion of its own resources left. Approval of an $18 billion contribution by the US to an overall $90 billion increase in the IMF's capital was only extracted from the Republican-dominated Congress with great difficulty by a weakened Clinton administration.

In the absence of such measures, the world's ruling classes are likely to be caught struggling between difficult alternatives. The plight of Japanese capitalism is a case in point. Since its formation in the summer, the government of Keizo Obuchi has been striving to come up with some solution to the crisis of the banking system, which is paralysing the entire economy. It lost two crucial months negotiating with the opposition over the fate of the bankrupt Long Term Credit Bank (a sound rule of thumb for investors: don't put your money into anything called 'long term'). The government didn't want it to go bust, because agricultural co-operatives are heavily represented among the bank's depositors and construction companies among its debtors. Both are important sections of the ruling Liberal Democrats' base.

But the problem lies deeper than mere crony capitalism. A thorough shakeout of the Japanese financial system of the kind demanded by the US Treasury and the IMF would force many banks and industrial companies into bankruptcy. The likely effect would be to drive the economy into an even deeper slump. But failure to restructure the banking system means that the present condition of paralysis is likely to continue. The same dilemma exists on a world scale. The speculative boom of the 1990s has left a huge overhang of capital which cannot be realised profitably. If it is destroyed through an extension of the present panic, then a 1930s-style depression is on the cards. But if piecemeal state interventions stave off such a collapse, the result is likely to be, at best, a sluggish and nervous world economy.

How severe the resulting downturn will be depends on a number of variables whose value it is impossible to predict with any confidence. A combination of more political fumbling and further economic shocks could precipitate the financial markets in a vicious downward spiral in which all the devices that fuelled speculation in the past now help to feed the panic. This scenario could leave the global financial system broken or paralysed, leading to a generalisation of the deflationary slump currently being experienced by Japan. Such an outcome is by no means inevitable. But even if state action is sufficient to prop the financial markets and stave off a 1930s-style depression, Europe and the US will probably experience shrinking output and rising unemployment, with the rest of the world suffering more severely, and enormous pressure being placed on capitalist political structures.

The political and ideological backwash

Political instability: The political effects of the crisis are already making themselves felt in East Asia. Mahathir Mohamad once said, 'Massive and rapid growth is a wonderful buffer. Like a river in flood it hides the rocks on the river bed'.[97] This is not only true of Malaysia. Throughout the region authoritarian regimes were able to contain significant social and ethnic tensions, as well as their conflicts with each other, thanks to the economic boom. But what happens when the growth stops? Then, to continue Mahathir's metaphor, the rocks below can hole and sink boats that had hitherto been swept forward by the flood.

'As things stand in September 1998, the possibility of a serious military eruption or shock in Asia cannot be discounted,' says Jean-Pierre Lehmann, professor of political economy at the Swiss Asia Foundation.[98] Already the region has had one major 'shock', with the revolution in Indonesia. This key development must, however, be considered in relation to the more general political instability of the system.

August 1998 marked not merely an intensification in the economic crisis. It also represented a qualitative increase in global political instability. Russia is the most obvious example of this change. Since the end of the Cold War, Western policy towards Russia has had two main thrusts—containing Russia strategically with a strengthened US-led military and political bloc (eg NATO expansion in Eastern Europe) and supporting Yeltsin economically and politically as the best hope of market capitalism in Russia.

The financial and political collapse at the end of August threw this policy into disarray. Given that, despite the decay of the past decade, Russia is still a military Great Power, the prospect is potentially horrific— 'Indonesia with missiles', as Martin Wolf put it.[99] The commentater Otto Latsis said that the Yeltsin regime has one last chance with the Primakov government: 'If this chance is not taken in a certain time it will be the end of democracy, the end of political liberalism and the problems will be solved by a Russian Pinochet'.[100]

The crisis of imperialist leadership: More generally, one can see developing a crisis of imperialist leadership, of which the G7's inept response to the August crisis is but a symptom. The US is indeed the sole superpower, far stronger militarily than any other state in the world. The US's share of world defence spending is larger now that it was in the mid-1980s, at the height of the Second Cold War, and is greater than that of the next six biggest Great Powers—Russia, Japan, France, Germany, Britain and China—combined.[101] But this military strength does not give Washington the political capacity to control a world heaving with crises.

Although the degeneration of the Clinton administration into a bedroom farce will make the situation worse, it is not the fundamental cause. Ever since the US became the main imperialist power at the end of the Second World War, it has relied not merely on its economic and military strength, but also on the construction of political alliances in order to secure its interests internationally. NATO is the most important example, securing as it does for the US the politico-military leadership of Western European capitalism.[102] But the Bush administration could launch the 1991 Gulf War against Iraq because it had created a coalition involving not merely European powers such as France and Britain, but also leading Arab states, notably Saudi Arabia, Egypt and Syria.

There are signs that, during the 1990s, the ability of US imperialism to carry its allies behind its major international initiatives has declined. The war crisis last February, when the US threatened to attack Iraq because of Saddam's opposition to the UN weapons inspection programme, illustrated the political limits of US power. Among the Great powers only Britain's Labour government supported Clinton. Russia, France and China opposed him, and Germany sat on the fence. In the Middle East even Egypt and Saudi Arabia, the major Arab states most closely aligned to Washington, refused to back the US war drive. Faced also with considerable domestic opposition, Clinton had to back down.

By allowing the Netanyahu government in Israel to sabotage the Middle East process, the US administration has fed a powerful anti-imperialist mood in the Arab world before which even the most brutal dictatorships have to tread carefully. Egyptian president Hosni Mubarak, who has used death squads to crush his radical Islamist opposition, said at the time of the February crisis, 'What matters is what public opinion in our country thinks. You will not find one [Arab] leader who is willing to say publicly, "We support the air strikes".' Crown Prince Abdullah of Saudi Arabia, the effective head of a regime directly dependent on US military support for its survival, went further, telling Secretary of State Madeleine Albright the following bedouin tale:

A livestock owner, he related, whose flock was losing a lamb every three or four days to a wolf, was persuaded to buy 20 fierce guard dogs to keep the predator at bay. But then he found he had to slaughter three or four lambs every day to feed the guard dogs. Pausing for effect the Crown Prince is then supposed to have gone on: 'At that point the owner of the flock decided to get rid of the guard dogs and co-exist with the wolf, as that was the least costly and perhaps the least dangerous course'.[103]

It is therefore hardly surprising that the US cruise missile attacks on Afghanistan and Sudan in August met with universal condemnation in the Middle East. The attack was in many ways an impotent gesture—as if destroying a harmless chemical factory and a few buildings would inflict serious harm on radical Islam. Meanwhile, acknowledging the lack of support revealed by the February crisis, the Clinton administration surreptitiously retreated from confrontation with Iraq over the weapons inspection programme.[104]

There have been other signs of US imperialism's slipping control in recent months. The war which broke out in the Democratic Republic of the Congo in early August is a very serious blow to US policy in Africa. Last year's overthrow of Washington's ancient and discredited client Mobutu was carried out by a coalition of states headed by Uganda which enjoyed considerable US support. On his visit to the continent in the spring of 1998 Clinton proclaimed an 'African Renaissance' in which liberal capitalism would bring a peaceful and prosperous future. Now the coalition has broken up, as two rival groups of states—Uganda and Rwanda versus Angola, Zimbabwe, Zambia and Namibia—fight over the corpse of the Congo while South Africa and the US wring their hands ineffectually on the sidelines.

Meanwhile troops are massing on the border between Iran and Afghanistan. The Taliban regime in Afghanistan has received backing from two key US allies, Pakistan and Saudi Arabia. Now it is drawing Iran into confrontation at a time when Washington has been trying to end its ineffectual policy of isolating the Tehran regime. The crisis threatens to destabilise Central Asia, a zone that has become of key importance to the various imperialist powers because of the race to develop the massive oil and gas reserves in and around the Caspian Sea. Elsewhere in the same region, Turkey, a key NATO ally and bound by a military pact to Israel, is threatening Syria with war unless it ceases to offer Kurdish guerrillas a safe haven.

Wars and revolutions: At the same time, the economic slump in Asia is likely to feed national conflicts in a region which has experienced a massive arms race in recent years. There are a number of long standing conflicts—for example, on the Korean peninsula, between China and

Taiwan, and over the oil rich Spratly Islands. Confronted with growing domestic social and political tensions, many governments may be tempted to try and maintain a degree of class peace by seeking external enemies. 'You're talking about haystacks that could go up in flames at any time,' says Lehmann.[105]

The economic crisis is therefore stoking up tensions among the world's ruling classes which are likely to lead to new wars and revolutionary upheavals. Indeed, it has already helped to initiate a revolutionary process in Indonesia that was the subject of detailed analysis in the last issue of this journal. Elsewhere in Asia, the most spectacular escalation of the class struggle has been in South Korea. Here the pattern has been less a spontaneous explosion than the continuation of earlier confrontations—above all, the mass strikes of January 1997. A critical factor here is the development, even in the semi-legal Korean Confederation of Trade Unions, of a trade union bureaucracy caught between pressure from below and the search to find compromises with the bosses. The outcome so far has been, a stand-off rather than a decisive victory for either side, but there are plenty more battles to come.

As the experience of both the 1930s and the 1980s shows, even a very severe economic crisis does not automatically lead to the a radicalisation of working class consciousness, let alone to successful socialist revolution. Nevertheless, one important factor in the unfolding crisis in the advanced capitalist countries is likely to be the revival of the organised working class in the US. The victorious UPS strike in the summer of 1997 has proved not to be a flash in the pan. The following summer saw successful strikes, most importantly at General Motors, but also at North West Airlines, Bell Atlantic and US West. Tight labour markets produced by a long period of economic growth have increased workers' bargaining power. But their greater willingness to fight also reflects the bitterness created by the past two decades of falling real wages, massive downsizing and the extravagant display of corporate greed.

Coming as it does after such a long period of defeat, this shift in the pattern of class struggle in the US is of enormous significance. It does not, however, mean US bosses have their backs to the wall. The 20 years when they had the initiative have boosted their confidence and refined their anti-union techniques. They took quick revenge for the UPS defeat by using legal pretexts first to remove Teamsters' leader Ron Carey from office and then to expel him from the union. As corporate profits come under increasing pressure from the developing crisis, US capitalists are likely to hit back hard. The prospect is for some bitterly fought class confrontations in the US.

Reformism in face of the crisis: Meanwhile, in Europe the victory of the

Social Democratic Party (SPD) in the German federal elections at the end of September means that, in most EU countries, social democrats are in office to greet the global economic crisis. This is an eerie repetition of the onset of the Great Depression, which began at the end of the 1920s with Rudolf Hilferding as German finance minister and Philip Snowden as British Chancellor of the Exchequer. The precedent is an ominous one, since the reformists were largely paralysed in the face of the interwar slump. Snowdon in particular distinguished himself with the rigidity with which he defended free market orthodoxy.

Gordon Brown is, of course, the Philip Snowdon of our days. Echoing Tory claims that rising unemployment was a 'price worth paying' for lower inflation, he declared that the slowdown of the British economy was 'necessary' to achieve a 'path of sustained growth'.[106] Tony Blair offered workers at the Fujitsu plant due to close in his constituency cold comfort: 'We cannot alter the conditions of the world semiconductor market'.[107] And, in an extradordinary interview on BBC Radio 4's *Today* programme on 30 September, he dismissed exchange controls as equivalent to protectionism, and defended financial speculation: 'It's easy to say on the rhetorical level, and no doubt you would get a good round of applause for it, that here's these young guys in braces destroying or making economies, but behind these are people making investment decisions about economies.'

New Labour, of course, represents the extreme right wing of European social democracy. Even Brown was forced to change his tune. After endlessly boasting about his 'prudence' in making the Bank of England independent, he launched a media campaign to pressure the Bank's Monetary Policy Committee into cutting interest rates in early October. Elsewhere in Europe social democratic governments espoused more open intervention in financial markets. The French prime minister, Lionel Jospin, sought to differentiate himself from the Blair-Clinton 'third way', saying, 'I am for the market economy as opposed to the market society'.[108] Although Gerhard Schröder, the new German chancellor, modelled himself on Blair, Oskar Lafontaine, SPD chairman and finance minister in the Red-Green government, dared to criticise the all-holy Bundesbank and advocated government intervention to stabilise the exchange rates between the major currencies. He made no secret of his commitment to a Keynesian policy of reflation.

What this will mean in practice is another matter. The SPD victory led to talk in the French Socialist Party about a concerted EU policy to sustain economic growth. But, as the Paris daily *Libération* pointed out, 'all idea of a recovery driven by the state is still considered faintly heretical the other side of the Rhine'.[109] In any case, control over monetary policy would soon be in the hands of a European Central Bank modelled on the Bundesbank. Already ECB president Wim Duisenberg has warned the social democratic governments not to tamper with the 'Growth and Stability Pact' which requires them to keep budget deficits to 3 percent of national income.[110]

The economic crisis is likely to shake the social stability of countries like France and Germany, where even the present 'recovery' has left the rate of unemployment at over 10 percent of the workforce. Europe's social democratic governments, brought to office by the rebellion against decades of neo-liberalism and economic stagnation, will find themselves caught between the workers who elected them and the demands of the financial markets and the central bankers that they stick to 'prudent', orthodox policies.

An Action Programme: All the same, a powerful ideological reaction to the blind worship of the market practised by Blair and Brown is setting in. It is a sign of the times that *Marxism Today* made a sudden reappearance in October 1998. The magazine had made its reputation in the 1980s by contradicting its title and denying the relevance of Marxism to the contemporary world. But in this special issue Eric Hobsbawm, Stuart Hall and others took Blair to task for failing to grasp the relevance of Marx's critique of capitalism. Having sniffed the way the wind was blowing ideologically, they identified themselves with the reaction against the market.

It is, however, important to understand that this reaction will not automatically benefit the revolutionary left. Mahathir Mohamad may denounce the failure of the free market, but that doesn't mean he wants to see workers' power in its place. The crisis will, in fact, produce a diversity of responses both intellectually and politically. Thus Larry Elliott calls for:

> ...a crash rethink of the basic tenets of economic orthodoxy. The Greens may be vindicated in their belief that reckless overproduction is putting the environment in deep jeopardy; the Marxists may be vindicated in their analysis that capitalism faced a crisis of profitability; the diehard Keynesians may be vindicated in their belief that unplanned and unregulated markets lead towards instability and disequilibrium.[111]

Plainly these different prognoses have quite different political implications. In particular, reformists of different kinds can agree that the market doesn't work but advocate not socialist revolution, but a return to the Keynesian policies of the postwar period or perhaps some more radical programme of nationalisation and state control of the kind advocated by Tony Benn and his supporters in the 1970s and early 1980s. On the far right, Nazis like Le Pen have their own critique of the market, which may find a larger audience if unemployment starts to rise again. Revolutionary socialists cannot, therefore, rely on the mere fact of economic crisis as a substitute for political argument and practical intervention.

It is important then that we go onto to the ideological offensive, to challenge the apologists for the market and to demonstrate the superiority of the Marxist critique of capitalism to orthodox bourgeois economics in both its monetarist and its Keynesian forms. But an abstract analysis, however powerful, is not enough. Particularly when involved in political discussion with other activists, socialists need to be able to show, concretely, how the workers' movement can impose a solution to the crisis.

The revolutionary socialist tradition contains some useful examples of how this can be done. The Third Congress of the Communist International, when it met in June 1921, faced a situation in which the immediate revolutionary wave following the First World War was beginning to recede and the workers' movement was facing an economic slump exploited by the bosses to win back the concessions they had been forced to concede at the height of the post-war class struggle.[112] Pre-war social democracy had been based on a 'minimum programme' of reforms which would improve workers' immediate situation while leaving capitalism untouched, and the 'maximum programme' of socialism. When forced to choose, the leaders of the Second International had opted for the former and, in order to rescue capitalism, even abandoned the most limited reforms.

The 'Theses on Tactics' presented to the Third Congress of the Comintern argued that the present crisis meant that defending the gains workers had already wrested from the bosses would require a struggle whose logic challenged the survival of capitalism. What was required was a programme that bridged the old minimum and maximum programmes:

The Communist parties do not put forward any minimum programme to strengthen and improve the tottering structure of capitalism. The destruction of that structure remains their guiding aim and their immediate mission. But to carry out this mission the communist parties must put forward demands whose fulfilment is an immediate and urgent working class need, and they must fight for these demands in mass struggle, regardless of whether or not they are compatible with the profit economy of the capitalist class or not... In place of the minumum programme of the reformists and centrists, the Comintern puts the struggle for the concrete needs of the proletariat, for a system of demands which in their totality disintegrate the power of the bourgeoisie, organise the proletariat, represent stages in the struggle for the proletarian dictatorship, and each of which expresses in itself the needs of the broadest masses, even if the broadest masses are not consciously in favour of the proletarian dictatorship.[113]

So rather than only issue abstract denunciations of capitalism and calls for socialism, revolutionaries should develop a system of concrete demands which reflect the immediate situation and consciousness of the working class. In conditions of systemic crisis, however, the struggle for these demands would clash with the very existence of capitalist relations of production. As workers became aware of this conflict, they would come to recognise, from their own experience, the necessity of socialist revolution. In this sense, such a programme involves 'transitional demands' that connect reformist and revolutionary consciousness.

Thus in June 1934, responding to the radicalisation of the French working class in the face of both the spread of fascism across Europe and the Great Depression, Trotsky published 'A Programme of Action for France' which advocated measures such as the abolition of business secrets, public control of industry, commerce and finance, the nationalisation of the banks, major industries, transport and insurance companies, aid for the small peasantry, reformed social services, the abolition of the police, political rights for soldiers, and self-determination for France's colonies.[114]

We do not yet face an economic and political crisis as serious as that between the wars. Nevertheless, the Action Programme recently put forward by the Socialist Workers Party sets out the kind of measures which could make up a solution to the present crisis—for example, nationalisation of companies that lay off workers; job-creating public works; an end to public spending cuts; a 35 hour week with no loss of pay; a decent minimum wage; full union rights; massive cuts in the military budget; and controls on capital.[115]

None of these measures explicitly challenge the capitalist system. Many are advocated by reformists and Keynesians. But, though they do not directly attack private property, the logic of workers' struggling for and implementing them would undermine it. A powerful workers' movement fighting for such an Action Programme would find itself forced by the bosses' reaction to choose between making even more radical inroads into the bourgeois system or acquiescing in the restoration of the priorities of capitalist profitability with all the suffering that would cause. Of course, these demands cannot automatically generate the struggle to achieve them. Nevertheless, this kind of Action Programme can act as a bridge in the socialist response to the crisis between abstract analysis and the concrete issues of the day.

A few years ago Tony Cliff said that the experience of the 1990s was like watching the 1930s in slow motion. All the same elements are present—economic crisis, class polarisation, the growth of the far right and the reaction from the left—but not yet with the same intensity and concentration as in the 1930s.[116] In the past few months the film has speeded up dramatically, in large parts of the world at least. This does not, of course, mean that the outcome need be the same as that in the 1930s. Fascism and imperialist war came after intense class battles—Austria 1934, France 1934-1936, Spain 1936-1939—in which the defeat of the left was far from inevitable. The scale of the present crisis, especially in Asia, starkly poses the alternative of socialism or barbarism. It is up to organised socialists to make the politics of revolutionary Marxism stronger and more rooted in the workers' movement across the world, and thus help to ensure the film ends differently this time.

Notes

1   *The Guardian*, 16 September 1998. I am grateful to Sam Ashman, Chris Harman Rob Hoveman, Michael Lavalette and John Rees for their comments on this article in draft.

2   'Please Don't Stop the Party', *Financial Times* (hereinafter *Financial Times*), 28 December 1996; see also 'The Ghost at Europe's Feast', *Financial Times*, 21 December 1996, and 'A Tale of Two Cycles', *Financial Times*, 23 December 1996.

3   C P Kindelberger, *Manias, Panics, and Crashes* (London, 1981), p5.

4   For an excellent set of detailed analyses of the East Asian crisis, see C Sparks, 'The Eye of the Storm'; Shin Gyoung-hee, 'The Crisis and Workers' Movement in South Korea'; and R Hoveman, 'Financial Crises and the Real Economy'; all in *International Socialism* 2:78 (1998).

5   *Financial Times*, 17 June 1997.

6   *Financial Times*, 6 October 1998.

7   M Wolf, 'Flows and Blows', *Financial Times*, 3 March 1998.

8   *Financial Times*, 7 Sepember 1998.

9   *Financial Times*, 28 August 1998.

10 J Rees, 'Indonesia: The Revolution's Next Step', *Socialist Review*, October 1998, p19.

11 *Financial Times*, 17 Sepember 1998.

12 *Financial Times*, 7 October 1998.

13 *Financial Times*, 9 September 1998.

14 *Financial Times*, 12 September 1998.

15 *Financial Times*, 1 September 1998.

16 *Financial Times*, 24 September 1998.

17 *Financial Times*, 24 August 1998.

18 *Financial Times*, 28 August 1998.

19 E Luttwak, 'Why Blame the Russians?', *London Review of Books*, 17 September 1998, p9.

20 *Financial Times*, 29 August 1998.

21 *Financial Times*, 18 September 1998.

22 *Financial Times*, 12 and 18 September 1998.

23 *The Observer*, 4 October 1998.

24 *Financial Times*, 17 September 1998.

25   M B Zuckerman, 'A Second American Century', *Foreign Affairs* 77:3, May/June 1998, p18.
26   Quoted in M Bygrave, 'From Wall Street to High Street', *Guardian Weekend*, 25 July 1998, p26.
27   *Financial Times*, 4 December 1997.
28   *Financial Times*, 26 March 1998.
29   *Financial Times*, 19 April 1998. A section of the reformist left, for whom South Korea represented an alternative, regulated, 'stakeholder' capitalism to the Anglo-American free market model, has effectively shared this analysis. Thus Benedict Anderson argues that the Asian boom depended crucially on political conditions, in particular US support for authoritarian pro-Western regimes during the Cold War, which no longer exist: 'From Miracle to Crash', *London Review of Books*, 16 April 1998. His brother Perry wrote recently of 'the worldwide triumph of capitalism' since 1989, and of 'the relentless advance of neo-liberalism through the Third World...a process now rolling through the last bastion of East Asia': *The Origins of Postmodernity* (London, 1998), pp135-136. Robert Wade and Frank Veneroso argue that the Asian crash has been exploited, and was perhaps engineered, by the US ruling class in order to destroy a rival model of capitalist development: 'The Asian Crisis: The High-Debt Model Versus the Wall Street-Treasury-IMF Complex', *New Left Review* 228 (1998). What this kind of analysis ignores is that productive capital in South Korea was already in crisis well *before* the financial panic began in mid-1997. And even if, as Wade and Veneroso contend on the basis of somewhat tenuous evidence, the US Treasury helped to encourage the Asian crash (see ibid, p20), the US ruling class now confront, like the sorcerer's apprentice, the consequences of their actions, which threaten to engulf them. These quasi-conspiratorial interpretations overestimate the power of US imperialism and fail to trace the roots of the crisis in the dynamics of the capitalist mode of production as a whole.
30   *Financial Times*, 5 September 1998.
31   *Financial Times*, 1 September 1998.
32   *Financial Times*, 2 September 1998.
33   J Geier and A Shawki, 'Contradictions of the "Miracle" Economy', *International Socialist Review* 2, Fall 1997, p7.
34   See P Krugman, 'America the Boastful', *Foreign Affairs* 77:3, May/June 1998, and R Brenner, 'Uneven Development and the Long Downturn: The Advanced Capitalist Economies from Boom to Stagnation, 1950-1998', *New Left Review* 229 (1998), pp235-251.
35   W Godley, 'Motor Starts to Sputter', *Financial Times*, 10 July 1998.
36   W Hutton, 'Bankrupt World', *The Observer*, 6 September 1998.
37   C P Kindleberger, op cit, p17.
38   See J K Galbraith, *The Great Crash 1929* (London, 1979).
39   *Financial Times*, 21 September 1998.
40   *Financial Times*, 15 September 1998.
41   *The Guardian*, 10 October 1998.
42   'The Fund that Thought it Was Too Smart to Fail', *Financial Times*, 25 September 1998.
43   J Plender, 'Western Crony Capitalism', *Financial Times*, 3 October 1998.
44   Quoted in J K Galbraith, op cit, p192.
45   K Marx, *Capital*, vol 3 (Moscow, 1971), pp516-517.
46   *Financial Times*, 10 October 1998.
47   *Financial Times*, 6 October 1998.
48   *Financial Times*, 12 October 1998.
49   D Hale, 'The Challenge Now is Trade', *Financial Times*, 7 November 1997.
50   *Financial Times*, 24 September 1998.

51 *Financial Times,* 6 October 1998.

52 *Financial Times,* 8 October 1998.

53 G Soros, 'Avoiding a Breakdown', *Financial Times,* 31 December 1997.

54 J M Keynes, *The General Theory of Employment Interest and Money* (London, 1970), p159.

55 W Hutton, *The State We're In* (London, 1995); and L Elliott and D Atkinson, *The Age of Insecurity* (London, 1998).

56 My understanding of the Marxist theory of crises is heavily indebted to the writings of Chris Harman, *Explaining the Crisis* (London, 1984), 'Where is Capitalism Going?', *International Socialism* 2:58 and 2:60 (1993), and 'The Crisis in Bourgeois Economics', *International Socialism* 2:71 (1996). A more popular version of this theory will be found in C Harman, *The Economics of the Madhouse* (London, 1995).

57 K Marx, op cit, p466.

58 Ibid, p476.

59 F Braudel, *The Structures of Everyday Life* (London, 1981), p112.

60 S Schama, *The Embarrassment of Riches* (London, 1988), pp343-371.

61 R Hilferding, *Finance Capital* (London, 1981), p135; see more generally Hilferding, Part II, and R Hoveman, op cit.

62 M Wolf, '1929 and All That', *Financial Times,* 7 October 1997.

63 For a comparatively straightforward presentation of the tendency of the rate of profit to fall, see A Callinicos, *The Revolutionary Ideas of Karl Marx,* 2nd edn (London, 1995), pp118-137.

64 A Shaikh and E A Tonak, *Measuring the Wealth of Nations* (Cambridge, 1994), p214; see also ibid, pp122-129, and Table 5.8. In another major Marxist study of US capitalism, Gérard Duménil and Dominique Lévy also write of 'the famous tendency of the rate of profit to fall' that its 'importance is confirmed by observation of the historical tendencies of the American economy,' *La Dynamique du Capital* (Paris, 1996), p233. Though Duménil and Lévy arrive at this conclusion on a significantly different theoretical basis from either Harman or Shaikh and Tonak, their analysis is particularly significant since Brenner draws heavily on their work in the article criticised below yet dumps the theory of the falling rate of profit.

65 Shin, op cit, pp40-44.

66 *Financial Times,* 6 July 1998.

67 R Brenner, op cit, p252. Brenner's detailed economic history of the three major Western capitalist economies (the US, Japan, and Germany) since 1945 is to be welcomed both for reinstating the rate of profit to its rightful place at the heart of any account of capitalist boom and slump and for the sustained critique it offers of the 'supply-side' theories advanced by both Keynesians and monetarists which explain the long period of crises and stagnation since the late 1960s on the basis of the success of working class organisation in pushing up wages and social benefits. Brenner's analysis is, however, badly weakened by his dismissal of Marx's theory of the tendency of the rate of profit to fall as 'Malthusian' because it supposedly 'posits a decline in profitability as resulting from declining productivity' (see pp11-12, footnote 1)—a perverse judgement (Marx actually argued the opposite) sustainable only because Brenner accepts the well known neo-Ricardian critique of the falling rate of profit: excellent rebuttals of this critique are to be found in C Harman, *Explaining the Crisis,* ch 1, in J Weeks, *Capital and Exploitation* (London, 1981), ch 8, and 'Equilibrium, Uneven Development, and the Tendency of the Rate of Profit to Fall', *Capital & Class* 16 (1982), and in E Mandel and A Freeman (eds), *Ricardo, Marx, Sraffa* (London, 1984). Brenner's own explanation of crises takes over one strand of Marx's theory—the contradictions which arise

when technical innovations leave capitalists who have sunk vast investments into outdated (or at least more expensive) technology confront more advanced rivals—but the result is at best one sided, and in some ways curiously arbitrary. Since Brenner has no way of explaining the overall trajectory of the rate of profit on a world scale, but rather treats it as the contingent outcome of variations in competitiveness between rival national blocs of capital, his massive account of the long downturn ends on a remarkably hesitant and uncertain note when considering the future of the world economy. Serious discussion of Brenner's undeniably important article is not helped by the absurdly extravagant praise accorded it in an editorial foreword which concludes, 'Marx's enterprise has certainly found its successor.' (pv) Hilferding, Luxemburg, and Bukharin, along with many other Marxist economists, are thus written out of history. This hype is reminiscent of the way in which, under Perry Anderson's editorship of *New Left Review* in the 1960s and 1970s, some continental theorist—Sartre, Althusser, Colletti, Timpanaro—would regularly be discovered and praised to the skies, only soon to be forgotten for the next one.

68   Commissioned for J Geier and A Shawki, op cit. I am grateful to Joel Geier for supplying me with the figures on which this graph is based.

69   Ibid, p12.

70   R Brenner, op cit, p191-192.

71   Ibid.

72   W Hutton, 'World Must Wake Up to This Disaster', *The Observer*, 30 August 1998.

73   W Hutton, 'Bankrupt World', op cit.

74   M Wolf, 'Threats of Depression', *Financial Times*, 26 August 1998.

75   For a critical discussion of the ECB and the ideology of central bank independence, see J Grahl, *After Maastricht* (London, 1997), ch 8.

76   See A Callinicos, 'Europe—the Growing Crisis', *International Socialism* 2:75 (1997).

77   J Sachs, 'Power Unto Itself', *Financial Times*, 11 December 1997.

78   *Financial Times*, 3 September 1998.

79   *Financial Times*, 23 September 1998.

80   *Financial Times*, 27 August 1998.

81   *Financial Times*, 11 September 1998.

82   *Financial Times*, 4 September 1998.

83   W Keegan, 'The Pearl Drops Out of America's Oyster', *The Observer*, 11 October 1998.

84   *Financial Times*, 22 September 1998.

85   L Elliott, 'West Must Find Cash for Global Fire Break', *The Guardian*, 14 September 1998.

86   On these earlier crises, see P Green, 'Debt, the Banks and Latin America', *International Socialism* 2:20 (1983), and C Lapavitsas, 'Financial Crisis and the Stock Exchange Crash', *International Socialism* 2:38 (1988).

87   *Financial Times*, 9 February 1998.

88   *Financial Times*, 27 December 1997.

89   *Financial Times*, 9 October 1998.

90   *Financial Times*, 15 September 1998.

91   W Munchau, 'A Leadership in Denial', *Financial Times*, 21 September 1998.

92   *The Guardian*, 14 October 1998.

93   A Giddens, *The Third Way* (Cambridge, 1998), p151.

94   S Edwards, 'Barking Up the Wrong Tree', *Financial Times*, 7 October 1998.

95   *Financial Times*, 22 September 1998.

96   W Hutton, 'Free Market Paradise Lost as Trauma Forces Rethink', *The Observer*, 4 October 1998.
97   *The Observer*, 26 August 1997.
98   *The Observer*, 7 September 1998.
99   M Wolf, op cit.
100   *Financial Times*, 18 September 1998.
101   G Achcar, 'The Strategic Triad: The United States, Russia, and China', *New Left Review* 228 (1998), pp97-98.
102   The recently published transcripts of the meetings by the key actors in the Kennedy administration during the October 1962 Cuban missile crisis show that a key constraint on US decision making, even in an area, the Caribbean, where it has overwhelming military superiority, was the need to carry Washington's European allies: see E R May and P D Zelikow (eds), *The Kennedy Tapes: Inside the White House During the Cuban Missile Crisis* (Cambridge MA, 1997).
103   D Gardner, 'Living With the Wolf', *Financial Times*, 17 Februrary 1998.
104   For more analysis of the current state of Western imperialism, see A Callinicos, 'A Century of Slaughter', *Socialist Review*, March 1998, and 'Licence to Kill', *Socialist Review*, September 1998.
105   *Financial Times*, 7 September 1998. The potential for military conflict in East Asia is explored in K E Calder, *Asia's Deadly Triangle* (Sonoma CA, 1997).
106   *Financial Times*, 24 July 1998.
107   *Financial Times*, 17 September 1998.
108   'L'Europe des Socialistes sera-t-elle Sociale?', *Libération*, 3 October 1998.
109   *Libération*, 2 October 1998.
110   *Financial Times*, 24 October 1998
111   L Elliott, 'How to Turn Recession into Slump', *The Guardian*, 17 August 1998.
112   For the background to the Third Congress, see D Hallas, *The Comintern* (London, 1985), ch 3.
113   J Degras (ed), *The Communist International 1919-43* (3 vols, London, 1956), vol I, pp248-249.
114   L D Trotsky, *Writings 1934-35* (New York, 1974), pp20-32. As the later history of the Trotskyist movement shows, the idea of a 'transitional programme' can be abused, but that does not mean that the basic concept need be rejected: see D Hallas, *Trotsky's Marxism* (London, 1979), and A Callinicos, *Trotskyism* (Milton Keynes, 1990).
115   *Socialist Worker*, 12 September 1998.
116   See A Callinicos, 'Crisis and Class Struggle in Europe Today', *International Socialism* 2:63 (1994).

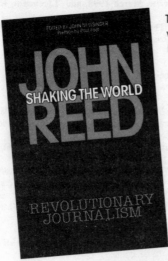

The Russian catastrophe

MIKE HAYNES and PETE GLATTER

'This is the collapse of a system.'
Svetlana Babayeva, 'The Inflation of Power', *Izvestiya*, 9 September 1998.

'We are watching the death of the Russian state.'
Paul Goble (director of Radio Free Europe/Radio Liberty), *The Baltic Times*, 1-7 October 1998.

The Russian ruling class has, in the last ten years, lost two empires—the outer empire, which included the whole of Eastern Europe, and the inner empire, the Soviet Union—and it has been unable to regain a firm footing even in Russia itself. It has lost its position as a world super-power and now, enfeebled, has to concern itself instead with such matters as the danger posed by atomic submarines rusting away in their berths. Its armed forces are a byword for desperate poverty, murderous bullying, unwillingness to serve and lack of will to fight. It has aban-doned the remnants of its Stalinist ideology without finding a convincing replacement. Its economy is in tatters. Much of its manufacturing industry has effectively ceased to exist. Its gamble on selling its raw materials abroad has failed, owing to the collapse in prices following the Asian crisis. Its financial system, such as it was, is a smoking ruin. It has defaulted on its external debt and its currency is an international joke. The state, with which it once identified itself, is fragmenting with at least

three unsuccessful attempts at stable government in 1998 alone. It has a
growing fear of revolt from below, with nightmarish memories of ragged
people looting the palaces in 1917; the Yeltsin family is not the only one
to be snapping up property abroad in case it has to flee.[1]

Neither Western nor Russian experts are clear about the nature and
causes of this crisis. Some have had their reputations destroyed like
Richard Layard, the leading British economist and adviser on the transition in Russia and joint author of *The Coming Russian Boom* which
'introduces Westerners to a Russia that is far healthier and more
promising than the one they have read about in the papers, and shows
how the greatest political-economic challenge of the post Cold War
world has become a resounding and exemplary triumph'.[2] Others have
become incoherent. Introducing his survey of Russia for 1998, Donald N
Jensen, one of the top officials of Radio Free Europe/Radio Liberty, for
many years a prime source of reliable information on the region (as well
as a notorious mouthpiece of Western propaganda), has concluded that
'no single description of the Russian political system seems adequate'.[3]
If such expertise, backed by considerable resources and experience, is
insufficient to arrive at a clear picture of the post-Soviet regime in
Russia, then ordinary people can hardly be expected to get much in the
way of clarity from the press, the radio and the TV.

A lot of the confusion has to do with traditional divisions between
left and right, especially during the period of the Cold War. Both right
and left shared the view that the Soviet Union was in some real sense
communist or socialist. The right tended to see it as a totalitarian state in
which the rulers sought to control every aspect of human life, while the
left found something progressive and admirable about the Soviet commitment to planning and state control. The left's illusions in Stalinism
have had little influence since the collapse of the Soviet Union, which
itself contributed to much of the left's rightward evolution. The right's
illusions in the accuracy of totalitarianism as a model of the Soviet
system have had a more lasting impact. Two points about the theory are
more important here. The first is that it was one of the few 'academi-
cally respectable' attempts to explain the Soviet system as a whole. This
partly accounts for the tendency among specialists seeking to explain
the decline and fall of the Soviet Union to fall back on totalitarianism
theory.[4] The second point is that totalitarian theorists made a qualitative
distinction between totalitarian regimes (ie Nazi Germany and the
Soviet Union) and non-totalitarian ones, even if the latter were as
unpleasantly authoritarian as Franco's Spain or Pinochet's Chile. If
there is a qualitative difference between totalitarianism and authoritari-
anism, then the gulf between a democratic republic like post-Soviet
Russia and the totalitarian regime which preceded it should have been

unbridgeable. Yet the fact is that the Soviet Union of Stalin and his heirs evolved into Russia and the other successor states of today without a major cataclysm—certainly nothing to compare with the huge changes which accompanied Stalin's own rise to power.

It was common ground among the theorists of totalitarianism that the way political power was organised was the fundamental feature of the Soviet system (much of the left too saw the role of the Soviet Communist Party, for example, as crucial to the progressive nature of the USSR). However, political power must always be seen in the context of the essential question: who controls the means of production, and what is the relationship between them and the actual producers? These relations of production constitute the economic base of society which underpins a particular political regime. This was the argument of those who insisted that far from being socialist the USSR under Stalin and his successors developed as a form of state capitalism. Forty years on, the same basic tools enable us to make sense of the transition from Stalinist to post-Stalinist regimes at a time when most of the left has thought it was witnessing the demoralising collapse of the 'socialist bloc'. As Alex Callinicos puts it:

> The social meaning of the East European revolutions was obscured by their most visible aspect, the collapse of the Stalinist one party states. But an economically dominant class must be distinguished from the specific political form through which it both secures its own cohesion and establishes its rule over society. The German bourgeoisie remained economically dominant throughout the twentieth century, despite a succession of changes of political regime—the quasi-absolutist Second Reich, the parliamentary Weimar Republic, the Nazi dictatorship, and finally the Bundesrepublik.[5]

The distinction between social structure and political regime is also vital to an understanding of the crisis of the ruling class in Russia today. It will be argued here that the ruling class has retained its control of the means of production since Soviet times, merely shifting its grip by means of privatisation. It has, as a result, continued to dominate the main successor state to the Soviet Union. But specific elements involved in the transition, especially the economic crisis and the loss of the Communist Party of the Soviet Union (CPSU), have disorganised and disorientated the ruling class and the state and have substantially diminished their internal cohesion with the result that Russia today is in the deepest crisis.

The problem of the transition from bureaucratic state capitalism

The essential problem of the Russian economy can be simply stated. To overcome Russia's historic backwardness, Russia's rulers, from Stalin onwards, drove the economy forward to compete militarily and economically with the West. The context and essential nature of this state capitalist industrialisation was well captured—despite his rejection of the theory—by Richard Sakwa:

> Political competition with the West was now transformed into an economic race, but one whose standards and measure of achievement were set in the West... In the context of socialism in one country Stalinism was primarily a war machine, with emphasis on heavy industry, a way of industrialising the country to sustain its military potential.[6]

For six decades this worked well enough for the Soviet Union to be able to defeat Nazi invasion and then maintain itself for nearly half a century as a credible opponent of the world's biggest power, the United States. But as the world economy grew more integrated in the post-war period the penalties of isolated industrialisation grew. By the 1980s the Soviet economy was clearly falling behind in this race.

In particular this centrally directed, military-industrialisation drive had important organisational and structural consequences for the Soviet economy which in the long run undermined its capacity to adjust and maintain its position. Organisationally Russia was run by the Soviet *nomenklatura*—the central political bureaucracy—which was to a large extent a managerial organisation.[7] From top to bottom, the CPSU, the key institution of the Soviet regime, spent more time and effort on the economy than on any other single area. A content analysis of the decrees issued by the Central Committee of the CPSU between 1966 and 1980 showed a 50 percent concentration on economic issues compared with 9 percent on foreign affairs and 8 percent on agitational work. As far as anyone can judge, this 50 percent figure is typical of the Party as a whole. 'Party secretaries receive medals and gold stars not for the state of party work in their area, or for the political maturity of the party organisation,' said Leningrad first secretary Gerasimov in 1988, 'but for record harvests and new factories'.[8] It was unusual for the Party's regional leaders (the pool from which Politburo members were drawn) not to have spent a considerable period in the management of one of their key local industries or of agriculture. This was even more the case in the huge new oil and gas regions of Western Siberia.[9]

However, the Soviet economy was not dominated by the regional Party leaderships but by upwards of 100 ministries, each of which controlled a particular branch of industry. These giant economic bureaucracies originally developed as the main mechanisms for implementing Stalin's forced industrialisation in the 1930s. The economic ministries were inured to

Stalinist motivation, priorities, methods and habits: military competition with the West; the development of heavy and military industry at the expense of infrastructure, social infrastructure and consumer goods and services; achievement of plan targets through the application of pressure and 'storming'; and, last but not least, empire building and the defence of one's own 'empire' against encroachment by other ministries. If the ruthlessness of the branch ministries mellowed somewhat over the years, then this was a change of degree, not of kind. Referring to the domination of the regional and local authorities by the ministries in 1984, the journal *Kommunist* revealingly commented on 'how the ministries have practically "torn asunder" entire cities such as Bratsk, Togliatti, Miass, each building "their own" part of town at a respectable distance from "the others".' Regional and local officials were locked into this industrial structure: 'Successful plan fulfilment by local factories was more important to them than a smoothly functioning regional economy'.[10] Despite much open debate and a clumsy attempt at reform the ministries retained their power until the end of the Soviet era.

Structurally, the conditions of enforced relative isolation also meant building up a parallel economy to that of the West. To achieve the same ends as the United States, Russia's rulers had to devote roughly two to three times the relative share of resources compared to the situation in the US. To support this it was necessary to develop a more powerful industrial sector than would be normal for an economy at the levels of development achieved by the former USSR. As economies grow there appears to be a broad but systematic relationship between the production shares of agriculture, industry and services. But because global competition forced the Russian economy to support an industrial base in advance of its level of overall development the gap between the actual industrial share and what would be predicted for a more typical economy at that level of development was considerable. In 1979, 62 percent of output came from industry compared to a predicted share of 40 percent. Resources elsewhere were squeezed, accounting for infamous weaknesses in housing, community services, distribution and so on. Even in the industrial sector much development remained significantly behind the West, operating at lower levels of productivity. Too often, from a global point of view, Russia had the wrong type of industry in the wrong place; plants were too large, turning out too diversified a range of products with equipment that was less efficient than that elsewhere in the world economy.[11]

By the mid-1980s it became evident that radical surgery was needed. Initially this took the form of Gorbachev's programme of *perestroika* or restructuring but as problems worsened the momentum developed to go further. When internal divisions at the top led a section of Russia's rulers to launch an unsuccessful coup against Gorbachev in 1991 they were motivated less by opposition to shifting to a more market economy than by their determination to limit democratisation and to hold on to as much of the Soviet empire as was possible.

Reformers on the other hand believed that it was necessary to weaken the ties of empire and to have a degree of democratisation to break the blockages in the bureaucratic system. With this they believed they could ensure that as much control as possible remained with those who had traditionally held it while allowing for some rejigging of the internal balance of power and some addition of new blood which could help reinvigorate the system. Secondly, they could keep their grip on power by ensuring that any protest from below was kept within bounds and diverted into harmless channels. Thirdly, they would redraw the lines of Russia's influence along its borders over the states that were now gaining nominal independence as well as over old neighbours using more flexible forms of informal domination.

None of these objectives have been attained successfully. Many accounts of what has gone wrong explain what actually happened as a battle between the reformers and recalcitrant forces of the old order and society at large. But, though there is some truth in this, to explain the development of Russia since 1991 solely in these terms is to accept the reformers' self-definition of the problems and to miss the wider logic of the changes. In fact it is now much clearer that the reformers were always operating at something of a tangent to the real processes of change. One obvious manifestation of this has been 'the revolving door' which has led to the recycling of the same personalities as government crises have developed since 1991 even as the policies they have been associated with have stuttered or failed.

When the Soviet pattern of development came under increasing pressure in the 1980s there were, in the abstract, essentially two ways out of the situation. One was to find the resources necessary to improve the productive structure of the economy. By massive planned external investment and assistance it might have been possible to renovate the decrepit industrial structures as well as to build up the missing parts of the economy, including a decent service sector, to answer the need of the population. The alternative was to allow the market to reallocate production by eliminating 'inefficient' production and pulling the economy backwards toward an integration into the world economy at a lower level of development.

The resources for the first type of transformation were in the West under the control of generations of leaders and businessmen whose concern with power and profit had already denied the poor of the world this kind of assistance. There was no chance therefore that this would be forthcoming to the former Soviet bloc and Russia in particular. Moreover even a more minimal aid programme geared to the direct reconstruction of production in Russia was seen to smack too much of Keynesian state control. Under the influence of neo-market liberal ideology, however, Russia's rulers believed, and were encouraged to believe by their Western advisers, that there was a third way. The hope was that the market could achieve the same ends of restructuring and refurbishment without a long run negative impact on Russia's position in the international division of labour. It was recognised that output would fall but it was hoped that this would be short lived and the economy would follow a U shaped curve—down and then up. And when it moved it up it would spring forward as the dynamism of the market was unleashed.

This idea rested on the mistaken view that what was holding Russia back was firstly state property, secondly bureaucratic management and thirdly insufficiently close ties to the world market. Thus the focus of discussion was the bureaucratic nature of the Soviet system rather than the contradiction between the internal economic structures and the wider logic of the world economy. The argument was now that if property relations were privatised, the market given greater scope in the economy, then managers would seize the initiative and use the world economy to pull the economy up. As Arthur Young, an 18th century contemporary of Adam Smith had put it, the 'magic of property' would 'turn sand into gold'. The writers of *The Economist*, never deterred by the experience of the real world, put it this way as late as 1995: 'The main problem with Soviet industry was not that it was short of technological expertise, or even capital. The ingredient it conspicuously lacked was competitive management'.[12] This can now be seen to have been a monumental delusion, though one that carried away the establishment, East and West.

Myths of the world economy

The potential of foreign demand to transform the Russian economy depended partly on the level of demand and partly on the capacity of the Russian economy to supply the goods demanded beyond its borders. The relatively slower growth of the world economy in the 1990s, even in its good years, has, however, limited external demand. Equally the inability of Russian producers, lacking substantial assistance, to produce the goods wanted at the price and quality required in the West has meant that demand has been weak. Even in the defence sector there have been enormous problems and Russia's share of the global arms trade is estimated to have fallen from around 35 percent in the 1980s to 10 percent in 1997.[13]

Beyond this the only sectors of the Russian economy that have been producing goods saleable in the world economy have been oil and gas and base metals. A simple test of the link between the world economy and the rest of Russian industry is the all but non-existent face of Russian goods in the West. Even the Lada, perhaps the most visible consumer face of the old Soviet system, has largely disappeared. If we look at the European Union we find that in 1996 the whole of the former USSR only supplied 4.6 percent of its imports and the share of manufactured products from Russia was around 1.3 percent of total EU imports.[14]

The overall level of foreign trade has fallen dramatically along with the rest of the economy. Economists distinguish between the volume and value of foreign trade. If the price of a commodity like oil rises or falls then the value of trade can change without the volume of oil traded necessarily changing. Table 1 shows that the volume of oil and gas traded with the West has risen, even as output of oil has been slashed and output of gas has stagnated. The value of this trade has fluctuated with the changing price of energy, rising (especially in 1992 and 1993) and then falling in 1997 and dragging the economy down with it in 1998. Beyond the oil, gas and metals sectors, trade volumes and values have fallen across the economy so that today the Russian economy certainly has no deeper trade relations with the world economy than it had earlier. Moreover the trade level today is to an extent inflated because what appeared in 1989-1991 as internal trade of the old USSR now appears as external trade between Russia and the newly independent ex Soviet states in the Commonwealth of Independent States (CIS).

One of the apparent peculiarities of this trade pattern which has confused many commentators is the way that Russia has managed to develop a considerable balance of payments surplus in its merchandise trade. Given the dire state of the economy this is the opposite of what might be expected. Imports should be being sucked in to replace the consumer and producer goods that domestic industry cannot produce. But although consumption imports have risen this surplus has grown in recent years to a considerable level. The major explanation for this appears to be that dollars earned in exporting are then taken straight out of the economy again as capital flight so that they are not available to pay for imports but only to build up the balances of Russian capitalists abroad.

This began before the collapse. It now appears, for example, that before 1991 the TASS wire service—supposedly representative of the Soviet regime—was insisting on its services in the West being paid for into a Frankfurt bank account. Then much of the Soviet gold stock appeared to 'vanish'. The outflow immediately intensified with liberalisation. One prominent Western adviser to the Russian government suggested that 'to judge from conversations with well informed businessmen and government officials, 10-20 percent of the oil and at least

TABLE 1: OIL AND GAS PRODUCTION IN RUSSIA[15]

OIL (MILLIONS OF TONNES)

	Total	Consumption	Non CIS export	CIS export
1988	568.8			
1989	552.2			
1990	516.2	310.0		
1991	462.3	296.0		
1992	399.3	276.0	66.2	67.4
1993	353.9	234.0	79.9	50.2
1994	317.8	196.2	95.4	32.8
1995	307.0	193.2	96.2	26.1
1996	301.2	184.0	105.4	20.6

NATURAL GAS (BILLIONS OF CUBIC METERS)

	Total	Consumption	Non CIS export	CIS export
1988	589.8			
1989	615.8			
1990	640.6	478.5	94.3	88.9
1991	643.4	475.0	90.0	92.2
1992	641.0	450.5	87.9	106.5
1993	618.4	453.6	96.0	75.4
1994	607.2	439.0	109.6	74.7
1995	595.5	407.2	121.9	70.3
1996	601.5	407.6	128.0	70.3

(including gas condensates)

one third of the metals exported from Russia in 1992 were smuggled out of the country. Naturally, the revenues from these sales stayed in bank accounts abroad'.[16] Since then the total scale of the movement is uncertain with a multiplicity of estimates for the years 1992-1996 ranging from some $61 billion to $89 billion.[17] In addition to this it is important to note that, as in much of the poorer parts of the world, debt repayments on official loans have continued to act as a further drain on the hard currency earnings of the Russian economy.

Capital flight is one way of putting into perspective the other great failure—the lack of foreign investment. So limited has been the level of inward foreign investment that it perhaps runs at less than 10 percent of the level of capital flight. To understand this investment failure it is important here to make two kinds of distinctions. The first is between financial aid to the Russian government and real productive investment. The second is between promised aid/investment and delivered aid/investment. Most of the huge figures talked about in the press represent financial assistance rather than investment. This is not directly invested in the productive structure of the economy but it is used to keep payments flowing around the state and financial systems and back to the West. Account then also has to be taken of the fact that much in both categories is promised rather than delivered.

The idea that foreign direct investment could transform the Russian economy was always a fallacy. The Organisation for Economic Cooperation and Development (OECD) countries undertake more than 90 percent of direct foreign investment. But 70 percent of all global foreign direct investment goes to the OECD countries. This helps explain why foreign investment has not transformed the lot of the poor of the world. It simply does not reach them. Moreover what investment does occur beyond the OECD is highly concentrated, 'almost three quarters of private capital to developing countries in the 1990s went to only 12, mostly middle income countries'.[18] There was therefore little chance of major flows to the former Eastern bloc. In fact cumulative foreign direct investment *in the whole of Eastern Europe* in the years 1989-1996 was around $44 billion. This sounds large but we can put it into perspective by noting that in the shorter period 1991-1995 cumulative foreign direct investment into Britain was some $86 billion.[19] Thus the people of Eastern Europe have received around 50 percent of the investment that foreign companies have made in Britain with its 58 million population. Of this $44 billion Russia got under $6 billion—half the investment in Hungary with its population of some 10 million or the equivalent of some 7 percent of British investment in 1991-1995. The whole of Russia has received no more than a reasonably sized development area in the UK and much less than London. Or, to put it another way, less than a quarter of what India received in the same period.

The story becomes worse if the geographical location of investment is explored. After an initial surge in investment linked to energy and resource exploitation which drew some resources into the provinces it has been Moscow and the central region that has received the lion's share of investment—more than 60 percent in 1995-1996. Even the second city, St Petersburg, has received little—less than 10 percent of the total in 1995 and less than 5 percent in 1996. Thus what foreign investment there is serves to increase the degree of uneven development in the economy as a whole.[20]

Nor do international agencies alter the picture. The European Bank for Reconstruction and Development is a source of both financial assistance and productive investment but what few of its loans have gone to production have been concentrated in gas and oil. Beyond this its flagship industrial loans include £17 million for a brewery and £29 million for a chewing gum factory![21] For all the talk, therefore, of foreign investment the reality is that 'all [foreign direct investment] is coming from people who really have no choice but to be here—like McDonald's—in order to sell their products'.[22] Thus, 'far from acting as catalyst to domestic economic recovery, the external regime with its reliance on primary goods exports heightens the susceptibility of the Russian economy to external shocks, reduces the potential for increasing competitiveness of manufacturers and entrenches sectional and regional elites'.[23]

The 'market' in Russia

The failure of the world economy to bring relief to Russia intensified the internal contradictions within the Russian economy. After the failed coup of 1991 Yeltsin was able to wrest control from Gorbachev and, as the Soviet Union fractured, he had support to begin a reform programme in the Russian Federation. In October 1991 the Russian Congress voted 876 to 16 for economic reform and in November 1991 Yeltsin appointed Gaidar as finance minister to lead the economic reform. The Gaidar group self-consciously saw themselves as a 'kamikaze cabinet' (their term). They assumed that their polices would produce 'creative destruction' and therefore 'the bigger the shock the greater the therapy'. Seeing themselves as engaged in an heroic battle for the soul of Russia they argued that it was only possible to jump over a chasm in one leap and therefore the most extreme policies were justified.

These policies had three major components—privatisation, liberalisation and macro-economic stabilisation. The problem was that these preceded any attempt to restructure Russian industry. The justification for this was that these policies themselves would force restructuring as enterprises would have to improve to survive. So long as this worked, privatisation, even if it was corrupt, would be justifiable because it would produce a new and more dynamic managerial class.

Observers inside and outside Russia therefore initially looked benignly on this process. Segei Kovalev, a usually reliable source, claims that Chubias, the man in charge of privatisation, said of what was happening, 'they steal and steal and steal. They are stealing absolutely everything and it is impossible to stop them. But let them steal and take their property. Then they will become owners and decent administrators of this property'.[24] In the West there was the same attitude. George Soros, the financier, argued, 'it's robber capitalism, it's lawless, but at the same time very vital and viable'. *The Economist* went even further arguing that in so far as the 'Mafia' had benefited from privatisation it was now time to legitimise it: 'The resulting gentrification of the mafia would be neither fair not pretty. But it would be part of the necessary process of capital accumulation'.[25]

In fact, of course, what happened was that monopolies used whatever power they had to try to hold on to their positions. Thus in January 1992 prices were freed from central control with the hope that as they rose this would in the short run absorb excess money and eliminate shortages by reducing demand (and increasing some supply), but instead they produced rapid inflation and monetary crisis. Parallel to this was the rapid development of a new banking system. At one point banks were being created at the rate of 40 a week and it seemed that anyone who had a minimal amount of capital (in 1993 $70,000 was enough) could start up a bank. The number of banks grew to over 2,500 in 1994 and then began to come down, as failures occurred and licences were withdrawn, to just over 2,000 at the end of 1996 and 1,800 by mid-1997.

These banks fell into four groups. Firstly, there were the branches of foreign banks. Secondly, there were the converted Soviet banks including the Central Bank, Sberbank (the savings banks in which what deposits the population had tended to be kept) and other parts of the old state banking system such as Mosbusiness Bank, Bank Vozrozhdenie, Promstroibank. Alongside these are a third group of 'pocket banks' created by large enterprises to act as their banking 'arms'. These range in size from the banks of the Gazprom natural gas monopoly of Viktor Chernomyrdin—the bizarrely named Imperial Bank (10th in size in 1997) and the National Reserve Bank (17th)—to minor outfits associated with smaller enterprises. Then fourthly there are private banks set up by individuals and groups. Neither of the latter two categories of bank have extended structures of branches or mass deposit bases since they were essentially created to meet specific needs or for market speculation. It is not surprising then that the OECD could say with typical understatement that 'commercial banks remain essentially inactive in the area of investment'.[26] In fact much of the banking sector depended in the first instance on foreign exchange speculation and this was soon to be supplemented by government bond dealings. They also acted as conduits by which loans coming into the country (including the huge loans from Western institutions like the World Bank and IMF) 'disappeared'. At the same time they were also one of the mechanisms by which capital flowed out of Russia to the West. And this is to say nothing of the more 'fully criminal' money laundering in which many were clearly involved. In addition, to survive the top banks also began to trade in political influence which they soon found so lucrative that the boss of Menatep unguardedly boasted that 'politics is the most profitable part of the business'.[27]

This was reinforced by the so called 'shares for loans' scheme which was a method of 'privatising' some of the jewels in the crown of Russian raw material production. In 1995 a group of Moscow banks proposed to the government that they could help finance the budget deficit if the government was prepared to back their loans with shares in the remaining state industries which included many of the 'jewels' controlling energy and raw materials. The Yeltsin government accepted the basic idea but insisted on an option to repay credits and, if they could not, that the enterprises should be competitively auctioned. When the government failed to find the resources to repay loans to the banks the result was high farce as the banks effectively auctioned off the enterprises to themselves. It was these shares for loans schemes that consolidated the role of the so called 'oligarchs', the leaders of the financial industrial groups (FIGs). One of these, Boris Berezovsky, in an interview with the *Financial Times* that caused ripples in Russia, claimed in 1996 that seven oligarchs now controlled more than half of the Rusian economy.[28] FIGs in their publicity handouts were likened to *Chaebol* in Korea and *Keiretsu* in Japan. In fact these FIGs would soon be exposed as weak and often parasitic structures behind which more powerful interests could operate.[29]

In the short run they appeared to thrive as an attempt was made to stabilise the financial economy after the initial inflationary surge. Inflation was forced down from some 2,600 percent in 1992 to 840 percent in 1993, 200 percent in 1994, 130 percent in 1995 and 20 percent in 1996-1997. As this happened Russia's image in world markets began to improve and in 1996 the Russian government was able to raise its first international loan and gain a listing on the New York stock exchange. In 1997 they could proudly boast a rating as a 'promising emerging market.' Yet all of this was accompanied by the continued decline in production. As Yavlinsky put it in the spring of 1998, 'We have low inflation, a low budget deficit, but we have almost no economic activity'.[30]

But this rouble stabilisation was a peculiar thing. Firstly the government borrowed enormous sums to achieve it. One part of this came from institutions like the IMF which was gradually sucked in to lending on an ever vaster scale. In July 1998 it agreed, for example, to new loans of $22 billion of which the first payment of $4 billion had been made when the economy crashed. The second source came from government issued short term loans, the treasury bills—the so called GKOs—and bonds or OFZs. These were sold to domestic and foreign investors at enormous interest rates. With the IMF giving its seal of approval larger amounts of speculative capital flowed into Russia, running for a time at levels that made real foreign investment look puny. But this state and private debt pyramid (linked in to the dubious domestic banking sector) depended on the state being able to maintain its payments.

Even without the impact of the Asian crisis this was a self-defeating process. In the first place the high interest rates acted as a further dead weight on investment. 'Who's going to invest in Uralmash when investors can make much higher returns on government treasury bills?' asked Korovin, the director of the Uralmash plant in the Urals.[31] Secondly, the pressure was on to cut back state expenditure and the state itself became as guilty of withholding wages as many private firms, which further weakened the chances of any recovery.

These pressures all added to the 'barterisation' of part of the economy as enterprises short of cash and depending on credit and mutual relations for their continued existence all did deals with one another. Thus the attempt to create a market economy perversely created a substantial barter economy. Barter rose from 6 percent of industrial output in 1992 to 9 percent in 1993, jumping with the drive to stabilisation to 17 percent in 1994, 22 percent in 1995, 35 percent in 1996 and an estimated 41 percent in 1997. These figures are for the whole industrial sector. But in parts of the economy the barter share was much higher—52 percent in chemicals and oil, 56 percent in metallurgy and 59 percent in building materials.[32] With this too went increasing delays in the payment of taxes.[33] At the start of 1998 only an estimated 15 percent of enterprises were paying their taxes in full and on time. Worse still from the point of view of ordinary Russians was the rising number of enterprises that delayed wage payments in whatever way they could.

On the other hand a third part of the economy, the dollar economy, remained immune from this. The size of this dollar economy remains difficult to estimate. Calculations by the state statistical agency put personal savings in dollars at the end of 1996 at over $100 billion—recalculations by other authorities put them at $11 billion—still the equivalent of 60 percent of rouble savings.[34] Most of these dollars were held by a relatively few Russians, the Manhattan elite as they are sometimes called, with access to foreign currency and the West. But where it has been possible—which is far from everywhere—ordinary citizens have also tried to convert some roubles into foreign currency as a store of value. Overall, even if we take some of the middle range estimates of the amount of dollars in circulation in Russia or stashed away somewhere, then it is quite possible that they exceeded the value of roubles in circulation *even before* the crash.

These problems were quickly exposed towards the end of 1997 when oil and other prices began to slide. Between July 1997 and July 1998 the price of oil fell by around a third. Income from oil and other raw materials fell to post-Soviet lows. Since oil alone accounted for some 15 percent of GDP, one quarter of government tax revenues and half the values on the Russian stock market, the implications of this were enormous. The Russian financial markets began to wobble in late 1997. The government pushed up interest rates to over 40 percent to calm nerves. In January and February the stockmarket dived again but recovered in March only to slide once more with interest rates being pushed up now to 150 percent. What was at stake here was not simply the economy. Writing in its Russian Supplement in the spring of 1998 a *Financial Times* journalist could describe how:

> The country's strongmen are beginning to crave political and economic stability. This small group of bankers, industrialists and regional bosses hit the jackpot during the mass redistribution of wealth that followed the collapse of communism. But now that the mass giveaway—which future generations of Russians may well condemn as the ripoff of the century—is over, Russia's winners are desperate to fully legitimise these gains.[35]

But central to this, ideologically and politically as well as economically, was financial stability. 'The strong rouble is for the establishment the sole achievement of seven years of reform. If it collapses, it's a political catastrophe for the ruling class,' Andrei Piontowski, a leading Russian commentator, told a Western journalist in the spring of 1998.[36] In March, Yeltsin, provoked in part by wanting to rid himself of a potential challenger, sacked the Chernomyrdin government to replace it with that of a young elite reformer, Kiriyenko. But Kiriyenko, perhaps suspected by those in power of doing too much, proved as unable as Chernomyrdin to hold things together, especially as the effects of the Asian crisis became more widespread. By August apparent pinpricks such as the announcement of the international financier George Soros that he had doubts about the stability of the Russian financial system could create havoc. By this point debt repayments were running at around 30 percent of the budget, but more importantly payments were coming to exceed the cash inflow of a government starved of tax payments. The crash came as August rolled on, despite desperate attempts to sell huge amounts of foreign exchange to shore up the value of the rouble. In the end it was to no avail and the rouble crashed—devalued by 40-50 percent; the state effectively defaulted on its debts; parts of the banking system collapsed and the government fell to give way to political demoralisation and short to medium term paralysis. Prices leapt for ordinary Russians who desperately grabbed what was left on the shelves of shops hoping to put their money into something of value as well as build up some stocks for the future. The whole system was now in turmoil.

How deep is the crisis?

The basic dimensions of the catastrophic declines in the real economy before the crash of the summer of 1998 are set out in Table 2. Some Western economists, dismayed at this picture, have tried to argue that these figures exaggerate the crisis because the old data inflated the levels of production while the more recent data fail to properly count all the new private production. Even if this is so, and a good case can be made that it is not, then the crisis of 1998 almost certainly wiped out a significant part of this shadow economy so that the declines indicated in this table cannot be that wide of the mark.[37]

The scale of the fall in gross national output registered in Table 2 is quite simply all but unknown in economic history save in the exceptional circumstances of defeat in war. And even in these exceptional conditions there are relatively few parallels. During the First World War, for example, output in Russia fell by 25 percent, during the Civil War it fell by 23 percent and during the Second World War it fell by 21 percent. Yet in the years 1992-1996 alone the decline was 28 percent.[39] After several years of hope that output would finally start a painful recovery it did rise by 0.4 percent in 1997. But even before the crisis of late August 1998 the preliminary figures for the first half year of 1998 suggested that output was down on the year before—the July 1998 figures suggested a fall of 4.5 percent for GDP, 9.4 percent for industrial output and 16.7 percent for agricultural production.[40]

Within the figures of total output it is industrial production which has fallen the furthest and its scale has gone far beyond what was predicted or what can be justified by even the most fervent free market ideologist. Moreover, the contraction has been evident even in areas that should be relatively strong. Despite the prominence of the oil industry, for example, oil production has fallen between 1988 and 1997 by around 50 percent, reflecting the depletion of fields, the lack of investment and a management more concerned to plunder oil resources than develop them. Gas

TABLE 2 : THE CRISIS OF THE RUSSIAN ECONOMY[38]

	GNP Index	Industrial Production Index	Agricultural Production Index	Investment as % of GNP	Prices % change	% Unemployed
1989	100	100			5.6	na
1990	97.0	99.9	100		92.7	na
1991	92.2	91.9	95	23	1,526.0	na
1992	78.8	75.4	86.5	18	875.0	4.7
1993	72.0	64.7	83	13	307.4	5.5
1994	62.8	51.2	73	11	197.4	7.5
1995	60.2	49.5	67.2	10	47.7	8.9
1996	56.9	47.0	63.8	9	17	9.3
1997	57.1	47.9	63.9	8	na	na

production has held up better but has been more or less stagnant over the period as a whole. Beyond this, old style Soviet industry has suffered, with mechanical engineering experiencing a huge contraction of some 70 percent between 1989 and 1996. But so too has light industry which might have been expected to expand, with falls greater than much of heavy industry. The OECD talks of the 'long free fall in light industry and food processing'—part of what used to be called group B industries.[41] As two Russian economists put it:

> Though much has been said about structural 'perestroika' (restructuring), no real changes have occurred in the increase in the specific weight of branches of group B. On the contrary...starting from 1992 their specific weight reduced significantly. At the same time the share of extractive industries increased from 15.5 percent in 1989 to 24.6 percent in 1996...the recession in manufacturing industry was bigger than in extractive ones...in almost all branches, the reduction of progressive types of production occurred at faster rates.[42]

In fact we can go further than this and argue that what has actually happened is what has been called a 'perverse restructuring' of the industrial sector. This makes little long run sense because it represents an accentuation rather than a resolution of the structural problems of Russian industry and can only compound the difficulties of recovery.[43]

This is not a 'healthy' process of deindustrialisation. What has occurred is qualitatively different from the process of Western deindustrialisation. There, the share of industry in total output fell but the absolute value of industrial output often grew, reflecting the fact that fewer workers and machines produce more, so enabling resources to be transferred to services. In Russia the opposite process has underpinned the deindustrialisation of the economy. Absolute industrial output has collapsed because fewer workers often produce less, so forcing up the relative share of the services sector.

There is a huge crisis also in agricultural production (which is also periodically affected by erratic natural conditions with 1998 threatening to be a very bad year). The agricultural disaster is one of the great secrets of the transition. Whereas the state of the Russian harvest was once the focus of much general reporting in the West, it has receded into the background, if not disappeared completely. Perhaps this is just as well, as Table 3 shows. The area of land under cultivation has fallen. While higher value food imports have grown to feed the rich, at the bottom of society the falling standard of living has reduced meat consumption at the same time as agricultural production has also been affected by much of the confusion and inefficiency affecting the rest of economic life. Livestock herds have dramatically declined, as Table 3 shows. The obvious comparison here is with collectivisation for which comparative data is provided in the last lines of Table 3.

For enthusiasts of the transition the one bright spot in this sorry tale is supposed to be the performance of the services sector. Anyone arriving in Moscow finds a city apparently bustling with life beneath a skyline of tall buildings overloaded with neon signs. This has led impressionistic commentators, including visiting economists and journalists, to speak highly of the transition. But two more sceptical commentators highlight the problem:

> Assume that one of the market economies of Western Europe were suddenly to cease all industrial and infrastructure investment, and to decide instead to use its resources for the exclusive purpose of building hotels, restaurants, casinos, cathedrals and luxury villas in and around the capital. In the short run, there would most certainly be an impression of astonishing wealth, but the longer term price to be paid would be disastrous. That obviously applies to Russia as well.[45]

In fact, telling though this comment is, it nevertheless still grants too much credit to the 'services revolution'. In reality there has been little

TABLE 3: SOME ASPECTS OF AGRICULTURAL PRODUCTION IN
THE RUSSIAN FEDERATION[44]

	1990	1991	1992	1993	1994
Grain Production (millions tons)	116.7	89.1	106.9	99.1	81.3
Potatoes (millions tons)	30.8	34.3	38.3	37.7	33.8
Eggs (billions)	47.5	46.9	42.9	40.3	37.5
Cattle (million)	57.0	54.7	52.2	48.9	43.3
Cows (million)	20.5	20.6	20.2	19.8	18.4
Hogs (million)	38.3	35.4	31.5	28.6	24.9
Sheep and goats (million)	58.2	55.3	51.4	43.7	34.5

	1995	1996	% Change 1990-1996	% Change 1928-1933 USSR
Grain Production (millions tons)	63.4	69.3	-40.1	-6.7
Potatoes (millions tons)	39.9	38.5	+25.0	-6.2
Eggs (billions)	33.8	31.5	-33.7	-67.6
Cattle (million)	39.7	35.8	-40.6	-44.3
Cows (million)	17.4	16.2	-21.0	-33.8
Hogs (million)	22.6	19.5	-49.1	-55.0
Sheep and goats (million)	28.0	23.6	-59.4	-65.1

absolute growth in the weak services sector. Employment in the credit and financial sectors expanded from 400,000 to 800,000 in 1990-1995 and in catering and retail trading it rose by 13 percent from 5.9 to 6.7 million in the same period. But employment in the rest of the services sector either remained stagnant or fell. Because overall employment declined by some 12 percent in 1990-1995 the relative stagnation of services caused its share of employment (and output) to rise but this is hardly the same as vigorous expansion. Even the small business sector— the hoped for breeding ground of a new class of entrepreneurs 'untainted' by the old order—has been largely stagnant. With major cuts in the level of mass consumption the capacity for sustained consumer growth is highly restricted and the accumulation of wealth in the hands of a relatively small group at the top can only provide the basis for a limited expansion for a few mainly dealing in Western goods.[46]

Table 2 shows the dire situation in respect of investment. No transition theorist has satisfactorily explained how a dynamic economy can be created by destroying investment. It should be remembered that part of the original driving force behind *perestroika* was the need to make more productive use of investment. But the fall in investment suggests that capital accumulation in production has all but been eliminated. This is confirmed by the figures on the age of Russia's capital stock. The average age of plant and equipment rose from 9.5 to 10.8 years between 1980 and 1990 but between 1990 and 1995 it rose from 10.8 to 14.1 years. If, in 1980, 35.5 percent of plant and equipment had been under 5 years old, the figure in 1990 was 29.4 percent but in 1995 a mere 10 percent. As a group of OECD authors put it, 'the ageing of plants and equipment is all the more ominous for the resumption of growth as large parts of even the relatively recent productive assets are technologically obsolete'. In the crucial oil sector, for example, half the pipelines are over 20 years old.[47]

Table 4 sets out some of the key indicators of the social impact of the economic crisis. Lack of space prevents us undertaking a full discussion of this data although we shall return to selected aspects of it later. Here, to the extent that these figures need commentary, we can simply quote UNICEF's monitoring reports lamenting 'the demographic implosion', 'appalling' numbers of excess deaths (1995); the 'staggering' fall in life expectancy for males (1996) which is now lower than in India; the 'tragic rise' in the deaths of young people including through suicide (1998) and so on.[49] We should also note that some of these series need to be treated cumulatively. Thus between 1990 and 1997 the rise in mortality over the 1989 level has led to between 2.6 and 2.9 million excess deaths attributable to the transition. It can similarly be estimated that the cumulative fall in births has been of the order of 4.5 to 5 million in the same period.[50]

The crisis of the ruling class

There is an irresistible body of evidence to indicate that the people now in charge in Russia are substantially the same as those who ran it in Soviet times. They were known collectively in Russia as the *nomenklatura*, and today people commonly refer to *nomenklatura* privatisation or to *nomenklatura* democracy. According to the Russian academic Olga Kryshtanovskaya, for example, members of the *nomenklatura* accounted in 1995 for 74.3 percent of the government and 75 percent of Yeltsin's presidential team.[51] Among the powerful regional elites who do much of the day to day bossing about, the proportion was even higher at 82.3 percent. Even in the new business elite the figure stood at 61 percent. These studies may even understate the level of *nomenklatura* persistence. Kryshtanovskaya herself admitted that this was the case when it came to the so called new business elite, 39 percent of whom seemed to have no connection with the old regime. She argued that even this significant minority was largely made up of trusted and authorised agents of members of the technocratic and economic *nomenklatura* who wished to remain in the background.

One of the interesting things about the different elite groups covered by these studies is the extent to which they share a common background in Soviet structures as opposed to the Communist Party or the economy. This was particularly true of the presidential team (63.6 percent) and the regional elite (78.6 percent). A shift from the Party to the Soviets began under Gorbachev and accelerated when the Party lost all credibility as a result of the abortive coup against Gorbachev in August 1991. A US researcher has referred to a typical scene from the autumn of 1991 as being 'the parade of former CPSU [Communist Party of the Soviet Union] regional leaders who "repossessed" their old office buildings in the name of the people and the soviets'.[52] Many members of the economic *nomenklatura* eventually chose the Soviets rather than the Party as the means for furthering their careers. Yeltsin himself comes from the construction industry in Sverdlovsk, a key region in the Urals. The Soviet background is therefore not so important in itself. But as a popular stepping stone in the careers of the upper classes it is an important indication of how the continuity between the Soviet and post-Soviet regimes was established.

Beneath these political changes privatisation, far from being the death knell of the old ruling class as free market economists would have it, actually became a crucial means for it to consolidate its economic grip.[53] Kryshtanovskaya describes a crucial example: 'A ministry would be abolished and in its ruins a business concern would be created in the form of a joint-stock company (same building, same furniture, same personnel); the minister would resign; the controlling parcel of shares would

TABLE 4: SOME MEASURES OF THE SOCIAL CRISIS IN RUSSIA[48]

	Gini coefficient*	Real wages (1989 = 100)	Birth rate (per 1,000)	Death rate (per 1,000)
1980	-	-	15.9	11.0
1985	-	-	16.6	11.3
1989	0.271	100.0	14.8	10.7
1990	0.269	109.1	13.6	11.2
1991	0.325	102.4	12.2	11.4
1992	0.371	68.9	10.8	12.2
1993	0.461	69.1	9.4	14.4
1994	0.446	63.7	9.6	15.6
1995	0.471	45.9	9.3	14.9
1996	0.483	52.0	8.9	14.1

	Marriage rate (per 1,000)	Infant mortality (per 1,000 live births)	Life expectancy (years)	
			Male	Female
1980	10.6	22.0	61.5	73.0
1985	9.7	20.8	62.3	73.3
1989	9.4	17.8	64.2	74.5
1990	8.9	17.4	63.8	74.3
1991	8.6	17.8	63.5	74.3
1992	7.1	18.0	62.0	73.8
1993	7.5	19.9	58.9	71.9
1994	7.3	18.6	57.6	71.2
1995	7.3	17.6	58.3	71.7
1996	5.9	17.0	59.9	72.6

*The Gini coefficient measures inequality on a 0 to 1 scale where 0 is perfect equality and 1 perfect inequality with 1 person having all the income

pass into the hands of the state, the rest would be distributed among the leadership of the ministry; as a rule, the second or third figure in the abolished ministry would become the head of the concern.'

This is, in fact, a summary of the 'privatisation' of the giant natural gas monopoly Gazprom, one of the largest companies in the world. The privatisation of Gazprom was organised by Viktor Chernomyrdin, the last Soviet minister of gas and the longest serving prime minister of post-Soviet Russia. As it was with Gazprom and Chernomyrdin, so it has been to varying degrees with other big business interests, especially banks and the big exporters of raw materials to which they are related. Despite the important, and recently disastrous, role of banks in Russia, their function has not necessarily been one of control over the big companies with which they have been integrating their operations. There is evidence that the top management in at least three of the six largest oil producers in Russia, including Lukoil, the largest one, bought their own companies, crucially in the 'loans for shares' auctions through the agency of banks to which they were allied.[54] In a fourth case, Yukos, the second largest producer, was officially taken over by the Menatep banking group which controls 85 percent of its shares. However, a study of banks in the Russian oil sector concluded:

> It is not strictly correct to say that the bank took over the company: rather, a mutually beneficial alliance was formed and confirmed in legal terms after a significant period of development... A full 70 percent of the assets of the Menatep group are now linked with Yukos. Total annual sales of the enterprises under Rosprom (Menatep's industrial investment arm) amount to somewhat more than $6 billion, of which $5 billion stem from Yukos. Yukos is a very large company and the size of the bank Menatep is not really of a comparable magnitude.[55]

These are—along with Gazprom—the largest exporters and the most important sources of hard currency earnings in Russia. They are, for what it's worth, among the most profitable firms in the country, the most closely allied to the state and the most privileged by it. Each has their 'curator' in government, a practice which has also spread to the regions. Thus, Yurii Luzhkov, the mayor of Moscow, represents a cluster of building, trading and financial institutions (most notably the Most group). Yurii Neelov, the governor of Yamalo-Nenets, the West Siberian region in which most of Russia's gas is located, sits on the board of Gazprom.[56] Leonid Polezhaev, the governor of the Omsk region, also in Western Siberia, sits on the board of Sibneft, the sixth largest oil producer in Russia. Sibneft owns the Omsk Oil Refinery, which is one of the largest petrochemicals plants in Russia, and its head offices are located in the region.[57]

A critique of research into 'elite continuity' by James Hughes, based on his investigation of seven regional elites, argues that the ruling social groups in Russia were even less variegated than Kryshtanovskaya and a co-worker in Britain, Stephen White, had supposed. For Hughes, the sub-national political elite, 'broadly uniform...in terms not only of occupational structure and status but also as regards age, gender and lack of overt party affiliation', is composed of an increasingly interlocked or integrated group of political-administrative and economic leaders. The old Soviet *nomenklatura*, he argued, has not only recomposed itself but has also succeeded in dramatically eclipsing other social groups in the elected regional assemblies—professionals, women, young people, employees and workers. He concluded: 'This is not the differentiated elite that one might have expected to emerge after a sustained period of democratisation'.[58]

It seems a matter of common sense to see continuity among the ruling orders as a stabilising factor in a time of change. Yet such continuity in post-Soviet Russia has gone hand in hand with a historically high level of conflict between different factions in the regime. The last days of the Soviet Union were preceded, indeed brought on by, an attempted coup by one part of the Russian-dominated Soviet leadership against the other (the abortive August 1991 coup against Gorbachev). Splits in the new Russian leadership soon developed and the most well known of them culminated in Yeltsin crushing the parliament by military force. Governments have swung between speeding up economic reform and slowing it down. In 1997, tension between the regional governors and the central authorities focused on an attempt to impose direct rule on the Maritime Province in Russia's far east via the newly appointed presidential representative, Viktor Kondratenko, who also happened to be the chief of the region's FSB (the renamed KGB). During the same year the Security Council gained and lost Boris Berezovsky, the 'oligarch' who fronts the Logovaz financial-industrial group (which includes Sibneft, Aeroflot and ORT, Russia's biggest TV station), one of Yeltsin's key backers in the 1996 presidential elections. This year two governments have fallen in a raging hurricane of financial and economic catastrophe—two and a half, if one counts Chernomyrdin's unsuccessful bid to get his old job back. The third, under the leadership of Yevgeny Primakov, a compromise figure, remains incomplete and unstable at the time of writing.

If post-Soviet Russia is essentially ruled by the same group of people as in Soviet times, why has so much of its brief existence been dominated by infighting among them? One answer is the apparently permanent and worsening state of economic crisis, to which none of them have a convincing answer. In the absence of effective measures promoting stabilisation and recovery, powerholders are reduced to bickering amongst themselves about their share of the take from a shrinking pot. Everyone fights harder over reduced rations, as Trotsky once remarked.

But the problem goes deeper than this. As we argued earlier, Russian state capitalism was an intensively bureaucratic and pyramidal phenomenon. But the collapse of the Soviet Union went hand-in-hand with the disintegration of the old Communist Party (the CPSU) which had structured ruling class relations into a hierarchy for 60 years. At the same time, there were shifts in the balance of power between different ruling class groups. Given implacable economic decline, such power shifts plus the loss of the CPSU destabilised relationships between the very groups of people most intimately involved in the business of the new state. They are a little like an officer corps which has survived some military disaster almost intact but at the cost of a breakdown in the chain of command, ie in the very thing that made it an effective officer corps. Their cohesiveness has deteriorated and the lack of clarity about who is subordinate to whom and to what degree has stimulated competing claims and conflict.[59]

Back in 1994, the writer and historian Yurii Burtin described the mentality of the Russian upper classes which had emerged from the demise of the Soviet state:

This is the phase of the omnipotence, one could say, the autocracy of the apparat and at the same time its hitherto unprecedented personalisation and personal freedom. Whereas in Soviet times it possessed power and property only on a corporate basis, 'as a class', now both have been largely decentralised and given out as personal property to every leading person taken separately—be it a director of a state enterprise, a regional or municipal administrator. You are free to use both as you see fit, at your own discretion, for nobody will tell you: 'You take not according to your rank,' nobody will take an interest either in your income or in the sources of this income.[60]

Burtin summed this up as a situation in which the ruling elite is simultaneously 'uncontrollable and omnipotent' and 'disunified...divided into parties, branches and factions,' producing 'leaders who are vying amongst themselves and are ready if need be to prove their supremacy by force.' He described *nomenklatura* democracy as having 'absolutely no chance of being effective and strong':

Expressing the contradictory interest of different groups of the socially irresponsible upper stratum, it is evidently doomed to live from one coup to

*another and from one 'charter of accord' to another. At the same time, it
keeps lying like a log on the path to genuine democracy, democracy for
everyone.*

It is the particular combination of continuity and change at the ruling
class level which is important. Had the *nomenklatura* been able to go on
ruling with its traditional mechanisms, it might have been able to cope in
the short term, perhaps even in the medium term, with the ups and downs
of different factions without too much in the way of internal disruption.
Had the *nomenklatura* been overthrown, then this kind of problem
simply would not have arisen. Ironically, the intra-class conflict which
typifies post-Soviet Russia is largely the result of a relatively peaceful,
relatively gradual process of reform which was initiated and led largely
from within the political establishment.

One aspect of this inability to sustain a clear command structure has
been the failure to establish a credible new political system through
which (and behind which) bargains can be made. The Soviet system was
always run from the top down and when Yeltsin and his reformers came
to power in 1991 they continued and in some senses reinforced this.
Supported by their Western advisers, they saw market reform and privatisation as a 'revolution from above'. When this programme generated
opposition which began to be expressed in the old congress or parliament Yeltsin resolved the conflict by sending in the tanks at the cost, on
some estimates, of around 150 lives in 1993. Out of this debacle came a
new presidentially driven constitution in which the new parliament (the
Duma) and the Upper House (the Federal Council) had limited powers.
Yeltsin and his group now eschewed building a party political base pre-
ferring alliances conducted inside and outside of the Duma to achieve
their ends.

But it is not only a matter of the political system itself. There has been
a major weakening of the Russian state machine. With the shift to the
market many of the economic control mechanisms of the old state, the
planning structure and many of the economic ministries, became redun-
dant. But the so called power ministries—the ministries of the interior,
defence, intelligence, special police, presidential security forces etc—
remained intact as the core of the state. However, their powers
effectively shrank and weakened as the crisis developed and they began
to lose control of social processes in Russia. Indeed, it was not always
clear what order should be imposed since the development of the market
often ran ahead of legislation so that much of what outsiders imagined to
be criminal in Russia (eg money laundering) is not necessarily against
the law since there is only very imprecise law to cope with it. The result,
as Kryshtanovskaya puts it, is that 'the law enforcement agencies, for all
practical purposes, themselves abandoned their task of safeguarding

private commercial structures'.[61] The best known result of this has been the rise of the so called mafia and crony capitalism. If the term 'mafia' in Russia applies to illegal organisations carrying out illegal acts, then just as important has been the growing role of legal organisations carrying out illegal acts whether it be in the form of the effective murder of workers in unsafe mines or factories, the scandals over environmental crimes that are producing horrific ill health in certain communities and so on. One manifestation of this has been the way in which state enterprises have been just as reluctant to pay taxes and wages as nominally private ones:

A general observation of the Russian state's policy in this period was that the government was unable to assert its nominal property rights over state owned assets. An evaluation from the state property committee showed that in most cases the management of government shares through the board representatives chosen had not been efficient, either for the state or for society at large. The biggest non-payers to the state and the biggest non-payers of salaries were precisely those joint-stock companies in which the state representative had responsibility for the management. Furthermore, the higher the position of the government representative, the larger the debt of the joint-stock company.[62]

The failure of the state is also reflected in the rapid growth of the private 'state', especially private security forces. Kryshtanovskaya argues that effectively all of these are run by former state security officials, 50 percent from the KGB, 25 percent from the Ministry of Internal Affairs and 25 percent from Intelligence and Armed Forces. But the difficulty is, of course, to separate out these structures from the illegal ones as merging can and does take place, especially in the financial sector. Leading criminals have even become deputies in the Duma where they can gain immunity from prosecution. One member of the Duma Commission for Human Rights, had, for example, previously been convicted of theft, armed robbery and rape.[63]

One of the paradoxes of bourgeois democracy is that much of its democracy has been achieved by struggles from below, primarily by workers but at times also including various middle class pressure groups and organisations. In the 1990s the buzz word for this was 'civil society'—what was needed in Russia was a network of independent organisations and groups that could express competing interests and both support state and government and pressure it in 'positive ways'. Yet just because the transition was a top down process, a non-revolutionary change with limited wider participation, no dense network of organisations emerged. Nor, of course, did the reformers always want them if they were likely to block change.

Nevertheless, something does exist. We will look later at the workers' movement and other movements which have offered opposition. In addition, there are groups that came together to oppose the Chechen war.[64] Some commentators see a wider difficulty in the fact that the middle class have also been victims of the economic decline. What was formerly known as the mass intelligentsia—teachers, doctors, workers in science and culture and so on have all found themselves victims of the maelstrom. As one Russian observer has put it:

> It is especially alarming that the 'centre' is dissolving. It seems to me that while some are going into business and becoming rich, a large proportion is becoming impoverished. The middle class is eroding... As we know, the middle class is the bulwark of any state—this is that stable group that is engaged in production, that makes it possible to master new technology, to treat and to teach people, to secure future development.[65]

In this situation we can see all types of shifts and splits occurring within the ruling class. The two most important dimensions of these—sometimes competing, sometimes complementing one another—are between the Financial Industrial Groups as power centres and regional divisions. The FIGs have effectively developed as political-economic empires to replace the former economic ministries. But the contours of their holdings vary. While some reformers opposed them for blocking competition others believed the talk that they would provide a new stable basis for economic and political power. In these terms Yeltsin even sent his adviser Sergei Shahkari to Japan to study the possibility of 'consolidating the ruling elite around a national revival and economic growth programme'. But as huge but weak empires they have depended on working political patronage and their links to the state.

The political patronage they have exercised has served to further weaken and destabilise the political system as client politicians and client media have vied to put the case for their 'employers' and stymie the plans of 'their' employers' opponents. The most recent turn in the crisis, by weakening the underpinnings of the system even more appears to have only accentuated this pattern.

A second aspect of this fragmentation has been the split on a regional basis. Russia has 89 republics and regions, each of which has two representatives in the Federation Council (the leaders of the regional executives and legislative bodies). The strength of Russian regional leaders has grown over time. In 1995-1996 regional governors were elected and this gave them greater standing against the central government. Then as the federal government weakened economically and financially their effective power increased further. This was especially true of the handful of regions which concentrated raw material exports and which therefore acted as 'donor' regions paying into the national budget, but it also applied more widely, especially where regional forces could find some other lever against the central government. Whatever their background, regional politicians no longer saw themselves solely as agents of the same central institution but also as representatives of regional forces. The situation, which has intensified since, was well described in 1994 by one influential provincial Russian leader:

> The centre, aspiring as before to the total control of the entire process of Russian existence, no longer possesses drive belts which would convey the impulses of its orders to the provinces. In the provinces, nothing at all remains of the archaic drive mechanism which existed in communist society. Rupture. Hiatus. The centre exists, the territories exist but effective connection between them is destroyed.[66]

It is this that underpins the fears that the fragmentation that has affected the old Soviet Union might affect the Russian Federation. There have been many regional threats to go it alone since the August crisis. This makes good politics in two senses. Firstly, manipulating, even inventing a 'regional consciousness' can help to consolidate political support. Prusak, the Niznyi Novgorod governor has said in these terms that 'we are not reds or whites but Novgordians.' Secondly, building up regional support can assist in putting pressure on the central government to win better conditions both for the region and the economic units based there. But to go beyond this towards a real fracturing of the state is an enormous step which at the moment is more talked about than real. Even if we leave aside the issue of the complexity of the bastard political forms and conflicts that this might bring there are two obvious difficulties. The first is that economically even the strong regions are less strong than they appear at first sight. The Tyumen oil region, for example, a major player given the concentration of so much oil wealth, has fractured internally. Although the oil interest has earned resources, it has done so on a basis of decline in production. Nizhni Novgorod has been widely advertised as a successful region. But this was a success which depended on foreign investment which, as we have seen, has been low overall. Moreover, it did not translate into the region having a markedly better system for the rest of its activity (for example, in the period where industrial production fell nationally by 55 percent, production in Nizhni Novgorod still fell by 50 percent) or in its pattern of government. This is the second crucial difficulty for regional leaders wanting to go it alone: 'Unfortunately, even progressive regions share the problems of conservative regions. It is not possible to be prosperous alone in a country where there are problems'.[67]

It is not suprising, then, that Russia's rulers do not know which way to turn. Even before the current crash, pessimistic commentators warned that 'in just less than six years, the country has made the dizzying journey from a superpower to a province that exports raw material and consumes foreign goods'. Unless decline can be halted the conclusion of this analysis would be that 'in the system of global distribution of world resources, Russia is with increasing confidence occupying the place 'allotted' it of a raw material appendage'.[68] At best this pessimism could be mitigated by the hope that uneven development would allow one or two areas and sectors to flourish in the midst of the remains of what was once a powerful state capitalism. In the depths of the crisis in August–September 1998 some even thought this option was not available: 'As of the start of September there's nothing to stabilise or reform. It's back to square one,' said one commentator.[69]

Every historian of revolution, whether Marxist or not, knows of Lenin's famous definition of a revolutionary situation as one where the ruling class cannot rule in the old way and the exploited classes are not willing to go on being ruled in the old way. We have seen how the first of these components are clearly in place in Russia as a result of the intensification of the crisis. What is missing is the second.

The crisis and the working class

The mass of the population have clearly been victims of the transition and it is not surprising that many look back nostalgically to the living standards that existed in what was once denounced as 'the era of stagnation'. But this is quite different to looking at the old Soviet system as a golden age or a viable alternative and it is quite striking that opinion polls do not show the mass of people supporting this argument. It would therefore be very dangerous if the left in the West were to fall into this trap.

Firstly, the fact that workers instinctively saw through the argument that the old regime was 'their' regime was reflected in the fact that they did not lift a finger to defend it—indeed it was partly their protests that helped to encourage its dissolution. Secondly, as we have seen, even from the point of view of some of the more backward sections of Russia's rulers there was no possibility of maintaining the old system as it was. To borrow an analogy—to a person on the verge of death the earlier stages of terminal illness look attractive but they are not viable places to which one can return. Thirdly, it was just this weakening of the old regime that gave Russian workers the confidence to begin to act for themselves for the first time for six decades. No longer in fear of automatic repression they have begun to reclaim a basic dignity. This was one of the reasons why the miners' strikes of 1989 were so important. For the first time for six decades Russian workers were able to experience the simple dignity of being able to march together in columns, no longer as a ritual, but for themselves, 'thousands of men still with coal dust under their eyes, in their pit helmets and working clothes'.[70]

This points to a fourth crucial point: the issue is not the 'troubles' that democracy brings but the lack of a real democracy, from the bottom up. The problem is the way in which the old rulers, with the connivance of their Western counterparts, have been able to hang onto power, however hamfistedly, and to milk the system for their own advantage. The way forward is not, therefore, back to some 'golden age' or in the direction of paternalistically welcoming some 'good' leader but to use the space that exists to build a real alternative from below. But while this is not difficult to see in abstract, in practice the difficulties are enormous both because of the legacy of ideological confusion left by the old order and the devastating impact of the worsening crisis.

A crisis on the scale of that which has wrecked Russia cannot fail to have a devastating effect on social relations. Mapping how this operates is not easy. The real incomes of those in and out of work have sharply fallen overall. The impact this has had on average consumption levels of foodstuffs is set out in Table 5.

However, wage differentials have also widened so that oil and gas workers now earn much more than, say, lowly paid teachers on 60-70 percent of the average wage. But even this can be misleading when workers are paid in kind or not paid at all for long periods (and then paid in money that has lost part of its value). According to one survey in early 1998, 75 percent of those interviewed had received their wages late in the previous year—38 percent by 1 to 9 weeks; 19 percent by 9 to 12 weeks, 12 percent by 13 to 24 weeks, and 6 percent by more than 24 weeks.[72] But, however qualified, evidence of the way in which the experience of the mass of the population is permeated by the punishing impact of crisis is to be found in every statistical series. Horror stories abound of the tragedies of individual lives. This has had an enormously debilitating effect. But this has to be set alongside evidence of enormous resilience too, a resilience which is not properly reflected in the pictures shown in the Western press and on TV, of occasional demonstrations in Red Square of old fascists and Stalinists with their pictures of the Tsar and Stalin.

To try to bring some balance to this we can crudely divide popular responses into three kinds. Firstly, what we can call 'opt out'; secondly,

TABLE 5: PER CAPITA HOUSEHOLD FOOD CONSUMPTION OF
SELECTED FOODSTUFFS (KG PER YEAR)[71]

Year	Bread	Meat products	Potatoes	Vegetables	Fruits	Milk products
1980	112	70	117	92	35	390
1990	97	70	94	85	37	378
1991	101	65	98	87	35	348
1992	104	58	107	78	29	294
1993	107	57	112	77	31	305
1994	101	58	113	71	30	305
1995	102	53	112	83	30	249
1996	97	48	108	78	31	235

retreat into 'defensive dependence'; and thirdly, and politically the most important, the guerrilla class war. These are not necessarily mutually exclusive categories. As circumstances change so people move between them and this gives rise to the possibility of greater social explosions as what Rob Ferguson has called 'the bitter fury of broken hopes' can turn outwards.[73]

Evidence of hopelessness that can lead people to 'opt out' can be found everywhere. The sense of uncertainty and lack of prospects is reflected in the collapse in the birth rate:

> People are uncertain about tomorrow—the last thing they want to do is to have children, it is a function of education combined with bad living conditions. People live badly in Somalia too but they do not stop having babies. Education seems to contribute to despair and hopelessness.[74]

Perhaps more graphic still has been the increase in suicide rates across all sectors of the population, though even in the depths of hopelessnes, some attempt can be made to retain a semblance of dignity. For example, one 87 year old in the St Petersburg region, not having received her pension, wrote out a note listing how much she owed and asking forgiveness for her debts before she hanged herself.[75]

But the evidence of 'opt out' is there in a no less wretched a way in the resort to the bottle which has been a characteristic of the past few years and which has destroyed so many lives both directly and indirectly. Just as it was said of the poor in 19th century Manchester that their quickest way of escape was the bottle, so today throughout Russia people have turned to vodka on a massive scale. One of the perverse effects of the crisis, even as real wages fell, was to push down the relative price of vodka. In 1984 a bottle cost twice the price of a kilo of sausages—by 1994 it cost a half. Supply also expanded as small scale producers tried to enter what appeared a lucrative market. If annual per capita consumption measured in terms of pure alcohol fell from 14.2 litres in 1984 to 10.7 in 1987 (with the Gorbachev anti-alcohol campaign) then by 1993 it had risen to 14.5 litres. Soviet men on average are consuming between one fifth and one quarter of a litre of vodka a day but often in the form of more intense weekly binge sessions. The result has been a huge increase in deaths, especially amongst middle aged men, which are directly and indirectly attributable to alcohol. The resulting fall in male life expectancy has been 'without parallel in the modern era'. Put another way, Russia now has 'mortality rates comparable with India or Guatemala'.[76]

The second reaction, 'defensive dependency,' reflects the way in which the crisis has forced the mass of the population to rely on their closest family and friends to develop survival strategies. With huge levels of poverty, falling (and intermittently paid) real wages and savings destroyed by inflation it has been necessary to depend more heavily than ever on family and friendship networks. Although wages might not be paid some benefits such as food can continue to come through the workplace. Beyond this the garden plot, once notorious as a symbol of the inadequate Soviet standard of living, is now even more important than ever to providing basic foods. Some workers, especially the more skilled, find second jobs (usually at lower skill levels). Still others engage in informal economic activity from women sewing to men helping in building and so on—the kind of strategies used by the poor the world over. Those in work have to help those out of work or too old to work to eke out their lives, those paid some kind of wages have to help those whose wages are 'delayed'. By the mid-1990s private transfers from those in work to those out of work were on one estimate taking up 40 percent of household income.[77]

Behind doors bolted against the world the family can come to seem a haven. Although the crisis has cut the marriage rate by nearly 40 percent between 1989 and 1996 it has not significantly increased the divorce rate, one of the clearest indications of this 'defensive dependence'. Such dependence is also thought by some analysts to be apparent in other relationships: 'It is widely believed that there has been an increasing commodification of sexual relations, with a tendency for the formation of temporary sexual relationships on the basis of a clear but implicit economic dependency of one partner on the other'.[78] But the capacity of the family to support one another is limited. A young working couple with depressed incomes can still help an aged parent, but a young working couple with several aged parents and children can mean abject conditions for all. And, of course, however much people may look to the family as a 'haven' the world cannot be bolted outside—it seeps in every way. UNICEF, for example, notes that in eastern Europe a similar pattern emerged but when some recovery began the divorce rate rose again suggesting, with some understatement, that 'the tendency to preserve marriages may have been a rational response to economic hardships and not a reflection of stable and stress free family life: therefore, welfare shocks may have heightened the risk of child abuse in the family.' To which we may add the risk of wife battering, grandparent battering and so on.[79]

At this point some observers have tried to extend this argument to suggest that this retreat into the personal has been paralleled by a retreat in the workplace where workers have gladly accepted alliances with their managers who, in trying to keep their plants afloat, appear to offer some defence against the crisis. Two US observers write that since the fall of Stalinism, the effect of greater labour market flexibility has been to increase working class dependency on management and that there still exists (although they see it as 'highly unstable') 'an accommodation between workers and managers'. This, however, is a dangerously misleading argument. It builds on arguments made in the past about the former Soviet regime where some thought that management-worker links meant that there was no clear structural class antagonism in that system. Now it is implied that the same is true of the new system.

But this is false in a number of ways. In the first place unemployment is rising, and many workforces have been drastically cut, suggesting that managers are prepared to take 'tough' decisions. Secondly, it is important to distinguish between what we can call 'a coincidence of interest' and 'dependence' and 'accommodation'. There is no doubt that on occasion managers and workers have tried to defend 'their' enterprises together, but there is nothing peculiarly Russian about this. This does not mean that structurally they have the same interests either in the long term or the short term. Were this the case it would be difficult to explain both the evidence of independent worker activity and management and local government opposition to it. It would also be difficult to explain the brutality that characterises managers' reactions to attempts by workers to show independence. One Russian commentator likens conditions of trade union organisation in parts of the country to those in the United

States before 1914, with unsympathetic local governments, local judicia-
ries and managements working together to sack workers and use
violence and intimidation against those who persist in trying to
organise.[80]

Contrary to those who emphasise dependence, there is ample evidence
of widespread (and up to the time of writing) growing class conflict in
Russia. More than this, it is clear that this conflict is occurring in a situation in which workers have few illusions left. Most notably the experience
of Stalinism taught them that this offered no kind of life. Equally there is
no evidence that workers are turning to the distorted remnants of that
system in the Communist Party or its allies. Secondly, the last ten years has
also taught that the market offers no solution and for the moment cannot
even guarantee the most basic needs for the survival of Russian capitalism.
Thirdly, the experience of transition has also ripped aside the credibility of
Russia's rulers and their institutions. This comes out in all the evidence of
opinion polls as well as that of actual behaviour as Table 6 shows.

TABLE 6: PERCENTAGE OF RUSSIANS SURVEYED EXPRESSING A
'COMPLETE LACK OF TRUST' IN GROUPS AND INSTITUTIONS IN
EARLY 1998 [81]

Army	44
Police	60
Private enterprise	70
Courts	50
Local government	61
Political parties	81
Newspapers	52
Trade unions	70
Privatisation funds	85
TV	53
Duma	70
Church	53
President	72

The actual number of recorded strikes is set out in Table 7, from
which it is apparent that most strikes have been small scale and local.
But they nevertheless exist, and while some of them have an edge of
desperation as workers go on hunger strike for back pay others show
more assertiveness. In May 1998 a wave of struggle over unpaid wages
spilt over into railway blockades. This so called 'railway war' began on
a small scale with miners taking action but soon attracted wider support
in parts of Russia—including from teachers and other white collar

workers. One account described these as 'a French Revolution style grab your pitchfork and go random spasm of raw underclass anger'. But for some it was more than this—one telling poster read, 'A hungry miner is fiercer than a Chechen'.[82]

The problem is that workers find it impossible at the moment to generalise from their struggles both in an ideological and an organisational sense. Ideologically, Stalinism broke any connection between the kind of activities that workers engage in on a day to day basis and the arguments of the socialist and revolutionary tradition about an alternative. At the same time organisationally it is proving immensely difficult for workers to sustain coherent organisation on a broad, long term basis. The larger trade union movement is part of the legacy of the state system. To survive it has had to take on some of the characteristics of more normal trade union work with its leaders oscillating like trade union bureaucrats of old. A smaller independent union movement also exists but neither organisation generates much confidence amongst workers, as is evident from the low opinion of them given to opinion poll questions. This helps to reinforce the localised and unorganised action but can also lead to it having a more explosive capacity to develop.

If building an alternative from below in Russia conceived in isolation may be a long and painful process, its progress may be accelerated by successful challenges to capitalism and the market elsewhere—challenges that can destroy the argument that socialism and Stalinism are automatically to be equated with one another. In the meantime this raises the alternative possibility that the solution to the crisis is some kind of coup.

Weimar Russia or what?

The apparent immediate future of Russia is indescribably grim. Output is falling, the value of the rouble has collapsed but yo-yos around its new lower level, inflation is likely to hit 400 to 500 percent by the end of the year, unemployment is growing, imports—including vital food imports—have been slashed, and Yeltsin is in semi-retirement after his failure to get the reappointment of the oil oligarch Chernomyrdin as prime minister. The new government instead is headed by Primakov, an old apparatchik, and Maslyukov, the former head of the Soviet central planning system, and Gerashchenko, the former head of the Soviet Central Bank, are now at the centre of economic policy. Even though they are very different people from a decade ago, it is a sign of the desperation that exists at the top that Primakov is asking for Western food aid as the threat of malnutrition becomes real for some sectors of the population.

To many commentators inside and outside Russia this raises the spectre of Weimar Germany. There too a weak democracy was hit by a

TABLE 7: OFFICIALLY RECORDED STRIKES IN RUSSIA IN THE
1990s [83]

Year	Strikes	Strikers (1000s)	Strikers per strike	Working days lost (1000s)	Working days lost per strike
1991	1,755	238	136	2,314	9.7
1992	6,273	358	57	1,893	5.3
1993	264	120	455	237	2.0
1994	514	155	302	755	4.9
1995	8,856	489	55	1,367	2.8
1996	8,278	664	80	4,009	6.0
1997	17,007	887	52	6,001	6.8
1998 (first quarter)	394	37	94	270	7.2

catastrophic economic crisis and then overthrown as important sections of the ruling class, to save themselves, swung behind an authoritarian coup.[84] The analogy with Russia is obvious and it can be made closer. The oligarchs, for example, appear to have been distributing their favours widely in order to have a foot in all camps should they need to take refuge in one of them.

But for the moment what appears to exist in Russia is what we can call a 'balance of weakness', which makes such a resolution more difficult. This does not mean that individuals may not be tempted to try their luck and go it alone but it does mean that the risk of failure is high. In the first place, all of the political forces in Russia today are weak. There is no political party which has a mass base, no political movement with a coherent and organised base from which it could try to make a bid for power.[85] This throws the onus more on the army. But here too there is disarray.

Analysing the situation from afar it is difficult to judge the nature of the debate in the upper sections of the army. However, it is clear that demoralisation is rife. 'The army is a mirror of the country as a whole,' said one member of the Russian Committee of Soldiers' Mothers (which tries to improve conditions of conscripts and opposed the war in Chechnya). 'If there is no order in the country how can there be in the army?'[86] Army numbers have been cut back from 2.8 million in 1992 to 1.7 million in 1996 and it was hoped to bring them down to 1.2 million by the end of 1998. This is a huge demobilisation. It occurs against a background of three effective defeats in the last decade—the retreat from Afghanistan, the loss of Eastern Europe and the humiliation in Chechnya. Chechnya should have been a way back for the army—a model military action in which it could demonstrate its power and that of the Russian state. 'A couple of hours and one parachute regiment' would be enough to bring the Chechens to heel, boasted the then defence minister, Marshall Grachev. In the event both conscript and elite forces crumbled against the Chechens and if Grozhny and other parts of Chechnya were left smoking ruins then it was still the Russian army that was humbled. Yeltsin could only extricate his forces with the assistance of a peace negotiated by his potential rival General Lebed. These humiliations were frontal attacks on army morale but it has also been drained away on a daily basis by the growing shortages of equipment, rations and housing. Discipline is often only held together by extreme brutality. Between January and September 1997 some 974 soldiers died, including 314 suicides. The draft is avoided on a mass scale—30,000 were reported to have dodged the spring 1997 draft. Sometimes officers can act on their own. Some (perhaps most) generals embezzle funds or sell big pieces of equipment while the rank and file sell small pieces. Other officers have to take local initiatives to survive, like the 60 homeless army officers in early 1998 who stormed a new apartment block to seize accommodation for their families in Khimki near Moscow. But in general it seems as if senior commanders try to forge links with regional rulers who can help find employment for troops and keep some resources flowing to feed the rank and file when the centre fails. As the crisis intensified in the early summer of 1998 the newspaper *Nezavismaya Gazeta* taunted that 'an army that gets fed dog food wouldn't give the president a full bore rifle today to prevent any coup'.[87] But to actively assist in a coup would require confidence that someone can supply more than dog food—or at least more dog food.

Beyond this, any prospective coup leaders have to ask themselves the question—which way forward? It is not obvious that anyone at the top knows the answer to this question. The immediate thinking of some liberals is that the economic question had more or less to be abandoned in favour of a struggle to preserve a modicum of democracy until after the next presidential election when it might be possible to rework institutions with less discredited forces and to construct a recovery programme. But the economy will not wait.

The result is a paralysing confusion evident everywhere. The new government brings together changelings from the old order and newer reformers but, at the time of writing, it has neither a stable composition nor a stable programme. Its own difficulties are compounded by the confusion at the global level. The IMF, which has both a general responsibility for the crash in the sense of its encouragement of the leap to the market and a particular responsibility in the way it encouraged the development of the short term bond market built round the ill fated GKOs, continues to chant its market mantra to the extent of insisting that 'free market' financial stabilisation is the only way to general stability. A government presiding over a people, part of which faces starvation, is instructed to cut expenditure and to raise taxes, even if it means more unemployment and the closure of much of the rest of Russian industry. Then, it is said, the magic will work and prepare the way for the next boom. But every time this step has been tried it has hit opposition from above as well as fears from below. And the famed world economy, the agent of salvation, is clearly now not exporting growth, but crisis. Not surprisingly, other voices attack these policies. One UN economist, Robert McIntyre, a UN based economist, trenchantly argued before the crash:

Russia's problem isn't that it doesn't bring in enough revenues to meet its obligations. Its problem is that it doesn't have enough cash to deal with all its financial market obligations. That's why the IMF has emphasised tax collection... The IMF bailout was really a subsidy for the oligarchs, for the Russian banks, and for the investors in the financial markets. And it was undertaken in a way that only made real economic problems worse... [The tax issue] is a false issue. Focusing on tax collection only provides an excuse to continue reneging on the responsibility to confront real problems.[88]

Since then other establishment voices have been raised arguing that Russia must 'put bread before theory'.[89] But how to do this is equally unclear because it is one thing to introduce controls in an economy that is failing, as in Asia, and quite another in one that is as wrecked as Russia. The current oscillation in policy will undoubtedly be a swing towards the state but this is likely to be just as incoherent and problematic as the swing to the market.

Predicting how this will be resolved is difficult. Certainly financially it appears inevitable that things will get worse before they get better. If the government cannot find a way out then the chances of further instability and fragmentation are high. If the situation remains too uncertain for a coup then an alternative is further fragmentation of Russia, not so much in terms of an explicit break up, but the development of stronger and politically erratic regional leaders.

To preserve something in this situation, much will depend on ordinary Russians fighting battles to preserve their standard of living and the minimal freedoms that they have gained since the collapse of the old Soviet Union. As we have seen, these fights are mainly local at the moment. But Russian workers have a history of revolt in which they have shown that they can move very quickly from conservative positions to much more radical ones even in very difficult circumstances. It would be a mistake to believe that in the absence of an organised nucleus of people arguing for an alternative from below that cannot not happen again.

Notes

1   J Meek, 'Yeltsin Ready for the Worst', *The Guardian*, 25 September 1998.
2   R Layard and J Parker, *The Coming Russian Boom* (New York, 1996).
3   D N Jensen, 'How Russia is Ruled—1998', 1 June 1998 (updated 28 August 1998), Radio Free Europe/Radio Liberty (Prague, Czech Republic); <http://www.rferl.org/nca/special/ruwhorules/index.html>, <http://www.rferl.org/nca/special/ruwhorules/elites-3.html>, <http://www.rferl.org/nca/special/ruwhorules/who-7.html>, accessed 8 September 1998. Earlier examples of expert incomprehension include this gem from a standard academic text, Richard Sakwa's *Soviet Politics: An Introduction* (London and New York, 1990), p59: 'Stalinism can be seen as a distinctive mutation of the Soviet system, neither inevitable nor immutable, but not necessarily avoidable either.'
4   See, for example, P Rutland, *The Politics of Economic Stagnation in the Soviet Union: The Role of Local Party Organs in Economic Management* (Cambridge, 1993), pp3-7; R Karklins, 'Explaining Regime Change in the Soviet Union', *Europe-Asia Studies*, vol 46, no 1 (1994), pp29-32, 42-43.
5   A Callinicos, *The Revenge of History: Marxism and the East European Revolutions* (Cambridge, 1992), p57; see also T Cliff, *Russia: A Marxist Analyis* (London, 1970).
6   R Sakwa, op cit, pp47, 59.
7   Ibid, p54.
8   P Rutland, op cit, pp25-26.
9   Ibid, pp197-205; T Gustafson, *Crisis Amid Plenty: The Politics of Soviet Energy Under Brezhnev and Gorbachev* (Princeton, 1989), pp305-306.
10   Quoted in P Rutland, op cit, p94.
11   See J Winiecki, *The Distorted World of Soviet-Type Economies* (London, 1988). This is a free market attack on the Soviet system but contains a mass of interesting information.
12   *The Economist*, 8 April 1995.
13   Stockholm International Peace Research Institute, *Handbook 1997*.
14   S Machold, 'Russia and the World Economy', Centre for Russian and East European Studies Working Paper No 5 (University of Wolverhampton, 1998).
15   OECD Economic Surveys, *Russian Federation 1997* (Paris, 1998), p224.
16   A Auslund, *Systemic Change and Stabilisation in Russia* (London, 1993), p9.
17   For a detailed discussion of the estimates of the scale of the problem and the different mechanisms through which capital has flowed abroad, see V Tikhomirov, 'Capital Flight from Post-Soviet Russia', *Europe-Asia Studies*, vol 49, no 4

(1997), pp591-615; L Abalkin, 'Begstvo kapitala: priroda, formui, metodui bor'bui', *Voprosy ekonomiki*, no 7, iyul' 1998.

18 J Stiglitz, 'That Elusive Blueprint for Debt Relief', *The Guardian*, 8 May 1998.

19 For figures for Western Europe, see R Barrell and N Pain, 'The Growth of Foreign Direct Investment in Europe', *National Institute Economic Review*, no 160 (1997).

20 OECD Economic Surveys, *Russian Federation 1997* (Paris, 1998), pp126-127.

21 By 1998 the EBRD had made loans to the value of £2.78 billion to Russia but had only distributed £950 million, of which £350 million had gone to the banks and £170 to gas and oil; *Sunday Business*, 6 September 1998.

22 *Financial Times*, 9 April 1997.

23 S Machold, op cit.

24 *Financial Times*, 1 November 1996.

25 *The Economist*, 8 April 1995.

26 OECD, *World Economic Outlook*, no 62, December 1997, p138.

27 Quoted in C Mellow, 'Clash of the Titans', *The Banker*, September 1997, p83.

28 'Moscow's Group of Seven', *Financial Times*, 1 November 1996. For a brief discussion of this self-proclaimed 'oligarchy,' see G Herd, 'Robbing Russia?', *The World Today*, April 1998, pp93-94.

29 As might be expected, some of the clearest accounts of the financial sleaze are to be found in financial magazines. See, in English, C Mellow, 'Rise of the Banker Clans', *The Banker*, April 1997; and the same author's 'Clash of the Titans', op cit. For a more academic account, see J Johnson, 'Russia's Emerging Financial-Industrial Groups', *Post-Soviet Affairs*, vol 13, no 4 (1997), pp333-365.

30 *Financial Times*, 15 April 1998.

31 Ibid.

32 S Aututsionek, 'Barter v rossiiskoi promuishlennosti', *Voprosy ekonomiki*, no 2, fevral' 1998.

33 *Financial Times*, 15 April 1998.

34 See *Russian Economic Trends*, no 1 (1997).

35 *Financial Times*, 15 April 1998.

36 *The Observer*, 31 May 1998. Piontowski was then director of the Strategic Studies Centre, Moscow.

37 Supporters of the transition put themselves in a contradictory situation since they simultaneously want to argue that (a) the crisis is not as bad as is made out because the statistics overstate it, and (b) too many inefficient plants are being maintained and therefore more output decline is needed! Livshits, Yeltsin's economic adviser, said that the spring 1998 Birmingham G8 meeting told him, 'We rate your programme very highly, but we'd rate it still higher if you'd just bankrupt something for once'; *The Observer*, 31 May 1998. In fact arguments for proposition (a) were often based on a priori reasoning and anecdote whereas a growing amount of research into measurement problems and the transition does suggest that the quoted figures are of the right order of magnitude. See, for example, D K Rosati, 'Output Decline During the Transition from Plan to Market: a Reconsideration', *The Economics of the Transition*, vol 2, no 4, December 1994, pp419-441.

38 UN, *Economic Bulletin for Europe*, vol 49 (1997); *Wirtschaftslage und Reformprozesse in Mittel-Und Osteurope*, Sammelband 1998 (Berlin).

39 This comparison was first made by a Russian economist, Andrei Illarionov. We are grateful to Mr Illarionov for confirming the details of the point with us. For comparison it should be noted that the GDP fall in the US between 1929 and 1933 was 30.5 percent.

40 *The Economist*, 22 August 1998; B Kagarlitsky, 'Dr Kagarlitsky Goes to Washington', *Focus on Trade*, no 29, September 1998.

41 OECD, *World Economic Outlook*, no 63, June 1998, p149.

42   N Ivashchenko and I Savchenko, 'Restructuring the Russian Economy: Problems and Tendencies, Centre for Economic Reform and Transformation Discussion Paper No 97/24' (Herriot-Watt University, 1997), p8.

43   See M Haynes, 'Eastern European Transition: Some Practical and Theoretical Problems', *Economic and Political Weekly*, vol xxxi, no 8, 24 February 1996, pp467-482, for an elaboration of some of these points in a the wider context of the East European transition.

44   Contemporary data *Russian Economic Trends*; historical data R Clarke, *Soviet Economic Facts 1917-1970* (London, 1972). The historical data is affected by boundary changes.

45   S Heldund and N Sundstrom, 'The Russian Economy After Systemic Change', *Europe-Asia Studies*, vol 48, no 6 (1996), p902.

46   OECD Economic Surveys, *Russian Federation 1997* (Paris, 1998), pp136-138, 246.

47   Ibid, p38.

48   Data from UNICEF, *Education for All? The MONEE Regional Monitoring Report*, no 5 (Florence, 1998).

49   UNICEF Poverty, *Children and Policy: Responses for a Brighter Future, Regional Monitoring Report No 3* (Florence, 1995); *Children at Risk in Central and Eastern Europe: Perils and Promises No 4* (Florence, 1997); UNICEF, *Education for All?*, op cit.

50   We have calculated these demographic losses by extrapolating the excess death estimate quoted by UNICEF in its 1995 report (p25) to the data contained in its 1998 report. The actual number of excess-deaths/reduced-births over 1989 levels is actually higher than these figures, but the estimating procedure makes allowance for the changing demographic structure that would have affected birth and death rates irrespective of the transition.

51   O Kryshtanovskaya, 'Finansovaya oligarkhiya v rossii', *Izvestiya*, 10 January 1996; 'Transformation of the Old Nomenklatura into a New Russian Elite', *Obshchestvehnye nauki i sovremennost'*, no 1 (1995), translated in *Russian Social Science Review*, no 4, vol 37 (July-August 1996), pp18-40.

52   G Helf, 'All the Russias: Center, Core and Periphery in Soviet and Post-Soviet Russia' (doctoral dissertation, University of California at Berkeley, 1994), p75.

53   This may have been the implicit intention. Formally the reformers, led by Chubias, agreed with Yeltsin that 'we need millions of owners, not a small group of millionaires'. But the real agenda was a concentrated capitalist class, although not one necessarily made up of the old leaders. See H Appel, 'Voucher Privatisation in Russia: Structural Consequences and Mass Response into the Second Period of Reform', *Europe-Asia Studies*, vol 49, no 8 (1997), for a discussion of the real strategy behind the rhetoric of the Chubias team.

54   V Kryukov and A Moe, *The Changing Role of Banks in the Russian Oil Sector* (London, 1998), pp22-41.

55   Ibid, pp27, 31.

56   P Glatter, *Tyumen: The West Siberian Oil and Gas Province* (Royal Institute of International Affairs Russia and Eurasia Programme Special Briefing, London, February 1997), p5.

57   V Kryukov and A Moe, op cit, p37.

58   O Kryshtanovskaya and S White, 'From Soviet Nomenklatura to Russian Elite', *Europe-Asia Studies*, vol 48, no 5 (1996), p729; J Hughes, 'Sub-National Elites and Post-Communist Transformation in Russia: A Reply to Kryshtanovskaya and White', *Europe-Asia Studies*, vol 49, no 6 (1997), pp1017-1036.

59   Among those who have drawn attention in passing to this phenomenon are P Hanson, *Regions, Local Power and Economic Change in Russia* (London, 1994), p15; and D N Jensen, 'How Russia Is Ruled—1998' (see Note 3).

60   Y Burtin, 'Emancipating the Apparat', *Moscow News*, 6-12 May 1998, p6.
61   O Kryshtanovskaya, 'Illegal Structures in Russia' (1995), translated in *Russian Social Science Review*, no 6, vol 37 (November- December 1996), p45.
62   V Kryukov and A Moe, *The Changing Role of the Banks in the Russian Oil Sector* (London, 1998), pp42-43.
63   O Kryshtanovskaya, 'Illegal Structures in Russia', op cit.
64   Sergei Kovalev, a leading Russian human rights activist, said, 'We turned out to be too exhausted, too broken and disillusioned, to shake Moscow with a 500,000 strong demonstration in the first days of the Chechen adventure as we did in January 1991 after events in Vilnius...but we turned out to be sufficiently sober not to allow ourselves to be deceived by the government', *New York Review of Books*, June 1997.
65   B Silverman and M Yanowitch, *New Rich, New Poor. New Russia: Winners and Losers on the Russian Road to Capitalism* (New York, 1997) pp29, 90-91.
66   L Polezhaev, *Vpered, na medlennykh tormozakh* (Moscow, 1994), pp61-62.
67   *Financial Times*, 9 April 1997.
68   Y Ryazhsky, 'Chernomyrdin's Ears', *Moskovsky Komsomolets*, 28 May 1997, p2, translated in *Johnson's Russian List*, 30 May 1997.
69   *The Guardian*, 9 September 1998.
70   R Ferguson, 'Will Democracy Strike Back? Workers and Politics in the Kuzbass', *European-Asia Studies*, vol 50, no 3 (1998), pp445-468. The argument of this section has benefited from an opportunity to discuss the first hand research in Siberia on which this is based without implying his responsibility for the use we make of it.
71   *Russian Economic Trends*, no 1 (1997), p81.
72   Centre for Policy Studies, University of Strathclyde, *New Russian Barometer: Getting Things Done With Social Capital*, vol vii (1998). Based on 2,000 interviews, February-March 1998.
73   R Ferguson, op cit.
74   Quoted in the *British Medical Journal*, vol 313, 17 August 1996.
75   *Isvestiya*, 9 September 1998.
76   M Ryan, 'Alcoholism and Rising Mortality in the Russian Federation', *British Medical Journal*, vol 310, 11 March 1995; US National Research Council, *Premature Deaths in the New Independent States*, 1997; D Leon et al, 'Huge Variation in Russian Mortality Rates 1984-1994: Artefact, Alcohol or What?', *Lancet*, vol 350, 9 August 1997; A Vishnevskii, 'Demograficheskii potentsial rossii', *Voprosy ekonomiki*, no 5, mai 1998
77   B Silverman and M Yanowitch, op cit, p23.
78   *Lancet*, vol 350, 19 July 1997, p213.
79   UNICEF, *Children at Risk in Central and Eastern Europe: Perils and Promises No 4* (Florence, 1997), p13; see also L Verikanova, 'Women Are Being Beaten', translated in *Russian Social Science Review*, vol 37, no 5, September-October 1996, pp17-24. One indicator of this is that child abandonment has become more common and there has been a 70 percent increase in the number of children institutionalised as well as a huge rise in numbers of Russian street children.
80   L Alekseeva, 'Unfree Trade Unions', *Moscow News*, 15-22 January 1995. For a horrific account of mining conditons which supports this, see M Tiabbi, 'Life in Hell', *The Moscow Exile*, no 42, 2-15 July 1998, http:www/exile.ru/feature /feature42.html
81   Centre for Policy Studies, University of Strathclyde, op cit.
82   On the railway war see RFE/RL Newsline passim; *The Moscow Exile*, 4-18 June 1998. Readers with access to the internet should check the 'Pay Us Our Wages' website maintained by the International Federation of Chemical, Energy, Mine and

General Workers' Unions which maintains a list of the bigger industrial actions as well as providing much other useful information.

83   *Russian Economic Trends,* no 3 (1997), p99; no 2 (1998), p78.

84   For an academic discussion, see S E Hanson and J S Kopstein, 'The Weimar/Russia Comparison', *Post-Soviet Affairs,* vol 13, no 3 (1997).

85   Dave Crouch, 'The Crisis in Russia and the Rise of the Right', *International Socialism* 66 (1995).

86   Quoted in *The Guardian,* 28 October 1996.

87   *Nezavismaya Gazeta,* 11 July 1998, quoted in *The Guardian,* 13 July 1998.

88   Quoted in M Taibbi, 'Exposing the Russian Tax Revenue Myth', *The Moscow Exile,* no 45, 13-26 August 1998.

89   M Desai, 'Russia Must Put Bread Before Theory', *The Guardian,* 21 September 1998.

Globalisation and the Third World

PHIL MARFLEET

False theory

The theorists of globalisation are in disarray. For a decade they argued that the world economy had changed fundamentally. They described a system integrated by the market and driven by capitalist energies which would deliver growth and unprecedented prosperity. A 'global era' of free flowing capital was to open up new opportunities for humanity as a whole, affecting economic structures and political, social and cultural life. One assessment saw this approach as so significant that it had become 'a key idea by which we understand the transition of human society into the third millennium'.[1] The globalisers predicted rapid development of Africa, Asia and Latin America, even arguing that divisions between 'developed' and 'developing' nations, 'First' and 'Third' worlds, would become less significant and eventually meaningless. In the face of renewed economic crisis, however, and of stark evidence of deepening inequalities and the immiseration of vast numbers of people, 'globaltalk' has become less strident. For one economic journalist writing in the wake of the South East Asian crisis of 1997, the model of globalisation 'has been recalled by the makers'.[2]

Globalisation theory maintains that all must benefit from recent changes. *The Economist*, house magazine of the global free marketeers, maintains that the world system now delivers 'more for all' and that vigorous growth in the Third World means 'it is the world's poor who will benefit most'.[3] Every index of economic and social advance, however, suggests otherwise. Among most of the 4.4 billion people living in Africa, Asia and Latin America life has become a *more* desperate struggle for survival. The United Nations Development Programme (UNDP) estimates that 840 million people are malnourished, the great mass of them living in countries of the Third World.[4] More than half the countries for which statistics are available do not have enough food to provide all their population with the minimum daily requirement of calories.[5] In some regions hunger has become far more general: across Africa the average household now consumes 25 percent less than in the early 1970s.[6] Between 1995 and 1997 only 21 out of 147 Third World countries recorded per capita growth of over 3 percent a year—the rate specified by the UN for reduction of poverty.[7] There are staggering inequalities. California alone has a gross domestic product (GDP) of equal value to that of China and India combined;[8] the wealth of the world's 15 richest people now exceeds the combined GDP of sub-Saharan Africa; the wealth of the richest 84 individuals exceeds the GDP of China, with its *1.2 billion* inhabitants.[9] There is no evidence to suggest that the 'global era' has brought prosperity, or even an alleviation of human suffering. On the contrary, even the conservative UNDP concludes that the picture is of 'a backlog of shortfalls and gaping inequalities'.[10]

In fact, such tendencies have been evident for years without troubling the partisans of globalism. Only the spectre of world recession has caused them to question aspects of the theory. Tracing this development during the 1997 financial meltdown, *The Guardian* noted that 'the great edifice, globalisation, had sprung a leak, but the problem was minor, mere running repairs.' A year later, it suggested, things looked different: 'No longer is it a case of damp in the attic: whole rooms are deep in rising flood waters...nobody knows for sure which country will be next...'[11] Responding to the mood of panic, Samuel Brittan of the *Financial Times* felt compelled to write a nervous defence of world financial institutions under the title 'Who's Afraid of Globalisation?'[12]

But if the standard model of globalisation has been 'recalled', so far it has merely been to modify the theory. For its partisans to reject the whole concept is almost unthinkable. Since the rise of neo-liberal economic theories in the late 1970s, notions of an expanding free market energised by unfettered capital movement have dominated approaches to the world economy and to development theory. Complemented by the idea of a 'New World Order' in which, after the death of 'Communism', capitalism advances under US guidance, globalisation theory has become a celebration of liberal capitalism. In the words of Yukuta Kosai of the Japan Centre for Economic Research, there has been 'a global shift' towards prosperity.[13] To question the core assumptions underlying globalisation is to question these principles—and much of the rationale for the world system.

Capitalism involves a restless search for profit by a class prepared to mobilise all means to pursue its ends and willing to elaborate all manner of rationales for its activities. In response to the world crisis of the 1920s and 1930s, for example, its ideologues abandoned a commitment to the free market in favour of highly restrictive state-based policies which willing academics soon justified with complementary theories. Such a turn is again possible but it is proving difficult for the globalisers to abandon ideas which have been presented both as a means of understanding the world system and as the blueprint for its future. In September 1998 the British economic journalist William Keegan reported on meetings of the Group of Seven (G7, the leaders of the seven dominant capitalist states) called to discuss problems of world recession. He noted their confusion and that of international financial officials, quoting one who admitted, 'We are worried. We are talking like mad to one another. But we haven't a clue what to do'.[14] Under such circumstances the globalisers are reluctant to desert their faith. Privately, noted Keegan, officials at the G7 summit recognised 'growing disillusionment with what "globalisation" has brought to some countries'. At the same time, such officials were not ready to abandon the orthodoxy: 'there are no signs yet of anything approaching a change of heart'.[15]

Academics who have criticised the theory show the same reluctance to question its key principles. On the one hand, it has become fashionable to recognise the 'downside' of globalisation. In a typical recent account, Nicholson writes, 'Globalisation has done little to remedy the big discrepancies in wealth in the world and may well have done things to make it [sic] worse'.[16] On the other hand, such 'revisionists' argue that globalisation is well under way or is accomplished, alleging that those who question the theory are unwilling to recognise changes in the world system: the expansion of market forces, the free movement of capital, and the enfeebled condition of nation states. They also stress the novelty and inevitability of these changes: for Gray, for example, 'The world historical moment we call globalisation has momentum that is inexorable'.[17]

In fact, the globalisation thesis *as a whole* is suspect. Investigation of the world economy today reveals a situation plainly at odds with the globalisers' main principles. Although some areas of the world economy show evidence of more fluid capital movement, some do not. Although, in one sense, there has been integration—nowhere is immune from the market economy—some regions formerly central to world capitalism have been driven to its margins. Some states are weak—but only in relation to very strong states which continue to dominate world affairs. The picture is one of unevenness and of contradiction. The notion that human beings are passive in the face of relentless economic and technological change is also false—as the upheavals in South East Asia have demonstrated. But most of its partisans remain firmly attached to the notion of globalisation. Their views are so much at odds with world realities that they should not be viewed merely as misunderstandings but as ideological constructions: ideas mobilised to justify and to perpetuate relations of exploitation and to assist in containing collective responses from below.

Global market

'Utopians': Recent attempts to modify globalisation theory attempt to rescue the perspective from its radical and Marxist critics, alleging that they focus on the wrong issues. Gray, for example, argues that sceptics have attacked only 'hyper-globalisation', what he calls 'the McKinsey worldview—the view of things propagated by American business schools'.[18] He continues:

> No one except a few Utopians in the business community expects the world to become a true single market, in which nation states have withered away and been supplanted by homeless multinational corporations. Such an expectation is a chimera of the corporate imagination. Its role is to support the illusion of an inevitable worldwide free market.[19]

To view globalisation in this way, it is alleged, merely sets up a straw man, a caricature of globalisation that is easily dismissed and allows critics to ignore the real changes in the world system.[20] But Axford, reviewing a mass of globalist literature, concludes, 'Much recent discussion of the world economy has emphasised the complete 'globalisation' of economic relations, so much so that there is sometimes an unquestioning certainty about the existence of a truly global economy'.[21] Hirst and Thompson concur: 'It is widely asserted that a truly global economy has emerged or is emerging'.[22] They describe the globalist orthodoxy: 'The world has internationalised in its basic dynamics, is dominated by uncontrollable global market forces, and has as its principal actors and major agents of change truly transnational corporations (TNCs), which owe their allegiance to no nation state and locate wherever in the globe market advantage dictates'.[23]

In addition, whatever realities it must confront, corporate capital wishes to propagate the view that there is a global rationale to its activities. Hoogvelt notes that corporations, international organisations, governments and the media increasingly speak as if they are operating within a 'globalised' system of freely flowing capital,[24] especially when they wish to discipline the workforce by reference to capital mobility and the 'portability' of jobs.

These ideas are far more pervasive than the global 'revisionists' suggest. Niall FitzGerald, vice-chairman of Unilever, one of the largest European corporations, argues that globalisation should be accepted 'as a fact of life'. We live in a "global village" of diminished borders, internationalism and free trade', he maintains.[25] Companies are not debating the existence of a global condition, 'they are responding to its effects'. Globalisation 'is simply the latest phase in the evolution of international business and the integration of the world economy'.[26]

Some former critics of the international system have been won to the argument that market integration is indeed a means of advancing human interests as a whole. Nigel Harris, a former editor of this journal who is now an enthusiastic globaliser, argues that capital circulates worldwide with increasing freedom, restrained only by the enfeebled state structures of an earlier era. Harris concludes that from within a new order, 'world interest and a universal morality are struggling to be reborn'.[27]

The conviction that world integration is imminent or even accomplished affects even those who continue to express hostility to international capital. William Robinson, for example, attacks the system as one that has produced 'prolonged mass misery and social conflict'.[28] He nonetheless accepts much of the globalisers' thesis. According to Robinson, transnational capital is a 'juggernaut'; it 'has been liberated from any constraints on its global activity' and has achieved 'total mobility and access to very corner of the world'.[29] This novel development is 'the fundamental dynamic of our epoch': 'In my view...activists and scholars alike have tended to understate the systemic nature of the changes involved in globalisation, which is redefining all the fundamental reference points of human society and social analysis, and requires a modification of all existing paradigms'.[30]

There is a further widespread assumption about the global market that corporate capital is keen to encourage, one especially relevant in the context of developments in the Third World. This is the view that world society should now be understood as a complex of consumers, a mass of individuals whose interests can be served uniquely well by the market economy. Absorbed from classical economics and applied by globalisation gurus such as management theorist Kenichi Ohmae, this sees a 'borderless world' in which freely moving capital interacts directly with the consumer. Encouraged by the spread of global media, it is said, there are unlimited opportunities to exercise choice: for the first time billions of people have direct access to goods and services.

This approach has had its impact on academic theorists of globalisation and of 'global culture'. Reviewing their perspectives, Waters comments that in a 'culturised' world economy, 'world class is displaced [sic] by a world status system based on consumption, lifestyle and value commitment'.[31] On this view, the integration of world society is a function of increased enthusiasm for shopping.[32]

In the real world

'Wastelands': These approaches are not the ideas of cranks from which more perceptive theorists of globalisation can now distance themselves. They are views widespread among theorists of globalisation which should be made to stand against the realities of the international political economy and the condition of humanity worldwide.

Rather than exercising new powers as consumers, billions of people are being forced to the very margins of the world system where notions of taste, choice and assertion of status must be measured against the imperative of survival. Over the past 30 years there has been a very rapid increase in global inequality. This is crudely estimated by the United Nations, based on differences between homogenised 'developed' and 'developing' nations. As we shall see, this is an inappropriate means of understanding world inequality but it does give 'headline' figures that stand starkly against the globalisers' account. Between 1960 and 1994 the gap in per capita income between the richest fifth of the world's people (most in developed countries) and the poorest fifth (most in developing countries) more than doubled—from 30:1 to 78:1. By the mid-1990s this trend was becoming more marked: by 1995 the ratio was 82:1.[33]

In 1997 the richest fifth of the world's people obtained 86 percent of world income; the poorest fifth received just 1.3 percent. Some 1.3 billion people subsisted on less than $1 per day—a life threatening decline in living standards since the 1960s. The trend was also accelerating: by 1996 no less than 30 countries showed an annual decline in the Human Development Index (HDI), which measures literacy, life expectancy, and access to health services, safe water and adequate food. Among 147 countries defined as within the 'developing' world, 100 had experienced 'serious economic decline' over the past 30 years.[34]

BASIC DEVELOPMENT INDICATORS—SELECTED COUNTRIES

	Human Development Index (HDI)*		GDP per capita (US$)	
	1970	1995	1970	1995
US	0.881	0.943	14,001	20,716
UK	0.873	0.932	8,463	13,445
S Korea	0.523	0.864	967	5,663
Malaysia	0.471	0.834	1,001	3,108
Brazil	0.507	0.809	2,049	2,051
Egypt	0.269	0.551	338	726
India	0.254	0.451	245	425
Zambia	0.315	0.378	440	257
Senegal	0.176	0.342	723	661
Haiti	0.218	0.340	333	231
Gambia	0.107	0.219	240	274
Niger	0.134	0.207	554	275
Sierra Leone	0.155	0.185	222	171

*HDI is calculated using figures for life expectancy, educational attainment (adult literacy and combined primary, secondary and tertiary enrolment), and standard of living (measured through adjusted income).

[Source: UNDP, Human Development Report 1998]

Some regions of the Third World, says the UNDP, have become 'economic wastelands'.[35] Most countries of sub-Saharan Africa are far behind the base growth level of 3 percent over a generation which is identified as necessary to reverse current trends to greater mass poverty. By 2030, the UNDP estimates, world GDP will more than double but Africa will experience a further sharp decline in its share of the world total: from 1.2 percent in 1997 to 0.4 percent.[36] The majority of Africans—some 500 million people—will be further marginalised within an increasingly productive world system.

Countries defined by the World Bank as being 'middle income' or 'upper middle income', and by the UN as showing 'high human development', have also shown a steep decline in living standards. In Latin America, long regarded as a relatively advanced region, the number of people living in poverty increased between 1990 and 1995 from 183 million to 230 million, or 48 percent of the continent's population.[37] In

1994 the UN's Food and Agriculture Organisation (FAO) estimated that 59 million Latin Americans were suffering chronic hunger.[38] In Asia, 40 years of growth among the Tiger economies had made them models for mainstream development strategists. Even before the meltdown of 1997, however, the World Bank noted 'a consistent pattern of poverty throughout the region', pointing out that a billion people lived below the poverty line, including over one third of the population of China. It also noted that inequality in a series of countries, especially in South East Asia, was becoming much more pronounced.[39] In October 1998 the United Nations Children's Fund (Unicef) reported that malnutrition in some parts of the region, notably Thailand, Indonesia and Malaysia, had reached proportions hitherto associated only with 'the benchmark of poverty—Africa'.[40] The Philippines government pleaded for massive aid from Western governments, arguing that that for the first time in 20 years, 'the war against poverty…is being lost [sic]'.[41] Even the Singapore government, which has long suppressed all 'bad news' stories, warned of the implications of unemployment and deepening poverty in neighbouring Indonesia, quoting estimates that half the Indonesian population of over 200 million would be below the poverty line by the end of 1998.[42]

In the worst affected regions such as the Horn of Africa and parts of West Africa, attempts to stimulate even basic development have largely been abandoned. Cox comments:

> *The perception that much of the world's population is not needed by the global economy seems to have been recognised implicitly (though never openly) by the principal world institutions. Policies to promote economic development have been very largely displaced in favour of what can be called global poor relief and riot control.*[43]

In these regions some states do not even feature in research programmes upon which organisations such as the UN base their analyses. Somalia, for example, has simply disappeared from the usually comprehensive UNDP reports.

Class: Inequalities are now so stark that even the UNDP recently reported the findings of *Forbes Magazine*, the US business journal, which in 1997 identified 225 people worldwide as having combined wealth of $1 trillion. Of these ultra-rich, over 60 percent were based in the most advanced industrial countries, including Japan. Of the rest, about half were based in Asia, a quarter in Latin America and the Caribbean, and the rest in Arab states, Russia and Eastern Europe. Two of the 225 were from Africa—significantly from South Africa.[44]

Although these figures show the usual weighting towards developed countries, they also show accumulation of wealth in the developing countries on a scale which was unthinkable during the colonial era.

Countries viewed as closely integrated into the most dynamic sectors of world economic activity show massive disparities of income. Panama is the location of a key artery of the world trade system and is categorised by international agencies as within the elite of developing countries. While the richest fifth of the population enjoys annual average per capita income of $17,611, the poorest fifth earns on average only $589. Over 25 percent of the population is below the internationally defined poverty line of $1 a day. At the other end of the scale, in Senegal, categorised within the group of least developed countries, the richest fifth have average per capita incomes of $5,010; the poorest fifth have a mere $299.[45] In nearby Guinea-Bissau, the figures are $2,533 and $90 respectively. Here 87 percent of the population attempts to survive on less than $1 a day and 40 percent are below the less testing local poverty line.[46]

All available evidence suggests that inequality is becoming much more pronounced. During the 1960s the poorest 50 percent of people in Brazil received some 18 percent of national income; by the mid-1990s the figure had fallen to 11.6 percent.[47] In Egypt, where the regime has been a Third World pioneer of neo-liberal economic strategies, 23 percent of the population was estimated to be below the poverty line in the late 1970s; by the early 1990s the figure had risen to over 40 percent.[48]

The human experience, far from being universalised by market forces, is more differentiated than ever. For billions of people the idea of choice, consumerism and 'value commitment' brought by a global era is fantasy. In fact, the recent phase of supposed global advance has brought increased suffering and uncertainty for far longer than the Great Depression of the 1920s and 1930s.

Combined and uneven development

Marx and the world system: We require an approach which can make sense of the partial and contradictory character of change. Such an analysis is to be found in theories of development pioneered by Marx and which were refined by Trotsky in the early years of the 20th century. Together with Marx's theories of the circulation of capital and of capitalist crisis, they allow an understanding of the dynamics of today's world system. They also make central the social forces that bourgeois theories including globalisation make irrelevant: the masses of the exploited worldwide.

The description of capitalist expansion by Marx and Engels in *The Communist Manifesto* captures the driven nature of the bourgeois project and its global implications:

> *The need of a constantly expanding market for its products chases the bourgeoisie over the whole surface of the globe. It must nestle everywhere, settle everywhere, establish connections everywhere...*
>
> *The bourgeoisie has through its exploitation of the world market given a cosmopolitan character to production and consumption in every country...*
> *All old-established national industries have been destroyed or are being destroyed. They are dislodged by new industries, whose introduction becomes a life and death question for all civilised nations, by industries that no longer work up indigenous raw material but raw material drawn from the remotest zones; industries whose products are consumed, not only at home, but in every quarter of the globe. In place of the old wants, satisfied by the productions of the country, we find new wants, requiring for their satisfaction the products of distant lands and climes. In place of the old local and national seclusion and self sufficiency, we have intercourse in every direction, universal interdependence of nations.*[49]

Marx, Engels and their co-thinkers anticipated that the expansion of capitalism from Europe would produce steady progress towards capitalist relations across what they called the 'colonial world'. Initially they expected that the immense economic and political weight of capitalism in the West would stimulate the growth of local capitalist classes, overwhelming rulers whose privilege rested upon pre-capitalist relations. As they wrote in *The Communist Manifesto*, 'The cheap prices of its commodities are the heavy artillery with which [capitalism] batters down all Chinese walls'.[50] In India, where British rule was bringing rapid change, Marx commented that England had 'a double mission...one destructive, the other regenerating—the annihilation of the old Asiatic society, and the laying of the foundations of Western society in Asia'.[51] The colonialists' were wholly self serving and, according to Marx, their methods were 'vile',[52] but in India he observed that they were transforming a largely rural society in ways that eventually would have positive outcomes. Atomised, self contained village communities were being brought together by railways, the telegraph and the centralising impact of a British army and administration. In the course of time, social forces capable of revolutionising Indian society would emerge, producing 'the only social revolution ever heard of in Asia'.[53]

Marx expected that this process would be general and that capitalism would spread worldwide, integrating every region into the system of commodity production. It would thus create the material, social and subjective conditions which would allow mankind as a whole to achieve revolutionary change and a classless society. In this perspective all countries would pass through the stages of development which had been witnessed in Europe, involving a relatively slow (though often traumatic) progress towards industrial capitalism—what might be termed (although Marx did not use the word) an 'even' development of the world system. As Marx spelt it out in the preface to *Capital*, 'The country that is more developed industrially only shows to the less developed the image of its own future.'

But this was not a one dimensional attitude to capitalist progress. During the European revolutions of 1848 Marx and Engels had observed the 'indecision, weakness and cowardice' of parties of the bourgeoisie.[54] This confirmed their notion of the 'permanency' of revolution, in which the most energetic and intransigent agents of change were the proletarians. Subsequent events gave them cause to modify further their approach to the bourgeoisie at a world level. The European experience was not simply reproduced worldwide, Marx noted. Colonial powers faced hostility from subject populations, to which they responded with savage repression. Capitalism could not even accommodate the aspiration for independence expressed by embryonic local bourgeoisies, which were not permitted to emerge as an independent force. Put another way, everywhere the bourgeoisie was weak and uncertain, and could not fulfill its 'historic tasks' of capitalist development. In the case of India, Marx noted, the interests of the masses would be best served by proletarian revolution in the West, or by an indigenous movement in which 'the Hindus themselves shall have grown strong enough to throw off the English yoke altogether'.[55]

This recognition of more complex and contradictory patterns of change was taken further in Marx's later writings. He suggested that in Russia, also a 'backward' country in which the embryonic capitalist class was weak, it might be possible to accelerate capitalist development. He observed that the Russian state had already implanted advanced industrial methods within a basically agrarian society, noting that 'the state has fostered a hothouse growth of the branches of the capitalist system'.[56] These observations were made as part of a debate with Russian populists which focused on other issues but reveal that Marx had become aware of processes by which, in non-industrial countries, changes introduced by capitalism could result in novel patterns of change. The most important of these was the co-existence of an 'implanted' modern industry with the traditional rural economy.

Trotsky's insights: Following the revolution of 1905 Trotsky made a far fuller analysis of developments in Russia. He focused upon the rapid growth of industry. This, he noted, had not emerged only or even mainly as the result of change pioneered by an indigenous capitalist class like those which had revolutionised society in Western Europe. Russian industry was largely of foreign origin and, encouraged by the Tsarist state, it had been implanted in the form of the modern, capital-intensive enterprise. He noted that 'capitalism in Russia did not develop out of the handicraft system [as in Europe]. It conquered Russia with the economic culture of the whole of Europe behind it'.[57] He continued, 'European capital projected its main branches of production and methods of communication across a whole series of intermediate technical and economic stages through which it had to pass in the countries of origin.' Change in Russia had therefore been abrupt: 'In a short period [European capital] converted a number of old archaic towns into centres of trade and industry, and even created, in a short time, commercial and industrial towns in places that had been absolutely uninhabited'.[58]

Trotsky described a process in which modern factories, transport systems and administrative structures coexisted with traditional practices: huge steelworks and engineering plants could be found alongside fields in which peasants still used the hoe. The pattern of development was uneven, combining the most advanced methods with traditional techniques, and producing centres of modern industry which were enclaves within a predominantly agrarian society. Trotsky observed that a journey from the countryside to the city could take peasants directly from the traditional context to the modern, from the isolation of rural communities to workplaces in which a new collective, the proletariat, was being established as a class with heightened expectations of change. He spelt out the revolutionary consequences, most importantly that the new working class had become a more coherent and powerful force than any other in the society, including the weak local bourgeoisie, and was destined to lead the struggle for socialist revolution. This was the basis for Trotsky's theory of permanent revolution, dramatically confirmed during the Russian Revolution of 1917.

Uneven development today: Throughout the 20th century, change in Africa, Asia and Latin Africa has been marked by a similar pattern of combined and uneven development. No region is untouched by market relations but these have not propelled societies steadily towards growth. Rather there are patterns of extreme unevenness. These are expressed, for example, in the 'megacities' of the Third World, in which modern industries have drawn in millions of former peasants to establish a new proletariat. At the same time, they are home to vast numbers of urban poor and to migrant labourers and semi-proletarians who may have a stake in the rural economy as well as in the city. Such cities also express the yawning gap which has emerged between the new bourgeoisies of such countries and the mass of the exploited, captured in the presence of five star hotels offering *haute cuisine* alongside slums in which vast numbers of people struggle for survival. Jakarta, Calcutta, Rio, Cairo, Bombay, Istanbul, Shanghai, Lima, Caracas and many others bear witness to the real outcome of changes in the world economy.

In most regions, change was at first associated with intrusion of Western capital. Later local bourgeoisies developed greater coherence and ambition but even in the post-colonial period they have remained junior partners in the imperialist system. Today some are little more than parasitical groups which share revenue from processing of local raw materials: the Gulf ruling classes, for example, are rewarded by the oil majors for guaranteeing access to the oilfields. Other ruling classes have made complex, sustained interventions in the local economy, largely through structures of the state. This is in general the case in the Newly Industrialising Countries (NICs)—a handful of states in which there has been relatively rapid industrial growth. They include Brazil, Argentina, Mexico, India, and the more celebrated East Asian 'Tiger' economies— South Korea, Taiwan, Hong Kong and Singapore. Alex Callinicos comments of the NICs:

> They are...cases of the process of uneven and combined development analysed by Trotsky in Tsarist Russia at the time of the 1905 revolution. They combine in equal measure 'advanced' and 'backward' features—advanced industry and authoritarian politics, a modern proletariat and great pools of misery and poverty. It is this combination which makes them liable to huge social and political explosions.[59]

One feature of change in the Third World which has invariably puzzled bourgeois analysts has been the level of engagement of urban populations and especially of the working class. Among a host of examples, the Chilean events of 1970-1973, the Iranian revolution of 1978-1979, the struggles in South Africa throughout the 1990s, and the Indonesian upheaval in 1998, have all demonstrated the specific weight of the proletariat within societies still regarded as in the process of development. Trotsky's analysis of class relations within the process of combined and uneven development has proved prophetic.

The NICs are examples of capitalist advance, but the unevenness of the world system has also produced the contraction and collapse of local economies. All states are subject to problems of world crisis but those most distorted by the world system are especially fragile. Thus, where capital has penetrated a country or region in order to extract specific raw materials or to use local resources for processing, changes in the world market or in local conditions can produce very rapid decline. In the mid-1970s, two thirds of exports from Chad were cotton; two thirds of Chile's exports were copper; and two thirds of Ghana's exports were coffee. In the same period, almost three quarters of Congo's exports were timber; a similar proportion of Cuba's exports were in sugar; and of Liberia's in iron ore.[60] Like scores of other countries, they faced immense difficulties during the world economic crisis of the mid-1970s. In some cases, local revenues declined precipitately. In Zambia, where the state had obtained half its income from the copper industry, a fall in world prices meant that by 1977 its receipts from this source had declined to nil, with catastrophic consequences for a population soon deprived by the state of subsidised basic foods.[61]

During periods of world recession, some vulnerable regions can be pushed to the margins of the system. Throughout the 1970s and 1980s countries of the Horn of Africa faced increased difficulties. They had not been exploited intensively for mineral or agricultural riches and were of little concern to the centres of world power. When wracked by repeated famines, mass movements of population and dislocation of economic and social structures, local states became highly unstable and by the early 1990s one state, Somalia, had collapsed. This produced a spectacle which might be a metaphor for world development: while millions starved in Somalia, in nearby Saudi Arabia, long exploited for its oil resources, billions of dollars were being mobilised to safeguard Western interests. There have since been further collapses in West Africa, where a series of local economies have become increasingly fragile and where in the mid-1990s the Liberian state disintegrated. Worldwide, more and more regions face such prospects.

The theory of combined and uneven development embraces change at a world level: it takes from Marx the notion of capitalism as an expanding system which draws in and integrates all countries, albeit in ways that Marx had not at first anticipated. It is a *global* perspective—but not one of 'globalisation'. It does not speak of positive integration by the market but of unevenness, inequality and asymmetry. Rather than harmony and increased prosperity we have more of instability, conflict and needless suffering. And rather than a passive population ready to accept its allocated role in global consumerism we have increasingly large and energetic political collectives, above all a more assertive working class.

Global capital

Forms of capital: The theory of combined and uneven development provides a framework for understanding the pattern of world development.

But just as Trotsky relied upon Marx's economic theories to explain the dynamics of Russian capitalism, so it is necessary to mobilise Marx's approach to understand recent developments in the world economy, especially the increased inequalities between the West and the Third World, and within Third World societies, that the globalist account conceals.

Marx's approach to the circulation of capital is vital to this task, especially because of the globalisers' insistence that capital flows are the key element in making a more equitable world. In classical economics and its contemporary variant, neo-liberalism, capital is essentially unitary, expressing itself as money, investment or profit and growing by virtue of entrepreneurs' energy in exploiting opportunities offered by the marketplace. In the globalist perspective, capital flows worldwide as the result of direct investment by companies and individual entrepreneurs, of activity on stockmarkets and commodity exchanges, and of initiatives taken by banks and finance houses. It is the change in volume and speed of capital transfers that makes for the more even distribution of capital and hence for globalisation.

Marx argued that capital can take *different* forms. He suggested that capital is not unitary, nor does it expand 'naturally' through the alchemy of the market. Rather, as he explained in Volume 2 of *Capital*, its form depends upon the human relationships involved in its mobilisation. Thus money and commodity capital are expressions of capital in circulation. Each, however, has its origins in productive capital, that which results from the direct exploitation of human labour. As Chris Harman insists, 'The point is important—money-capital often seems to be the "pure" form of capital, the form in which the self expansion of value is most vividly to be seen. But like the other forms of capital, it is in reality, as Marx put it, "not a thing but a relation", a relation which involves the exploitation of people at the point of production'.[62]

Identification of different forms of capital does not mean that they exist wholly independently: the process of accumulation involves many changes from one form to another. Production, which is at the core of the capitalist economy, requires that money-capital is used to buy machinery, materials and labour; and production itself brings into being commodities, which are in turn exchanged for money. But money can be moved through the system far more quickly than capital in form of material objects—machines, production lines, transport systems, etc. This is especially important in the context of credit. Banks and finance houses have emerged through the efforts of capitalists to benefit from situations in which they have profit to invest—but not necessarily enough to invest immediately in productive projects such as new factories or machinery. They may therefore lend what they have in hand to other capitalists, usually through banks. When they need to mobilise large sums they apply to banks for loans. In effect, the loan is an advance to the capitalist on the expectation of later realisation of surplus value through direct exploitation. It is in this context that speculation takes place, as capitalists gamble on anticipated profits, often using credit, and hoping to drive up prices in the process.

The distinction between forms of capital is of special significance in periods of slump. Faced with this prospect some capitalists may mobilise more of their resources in the form of money or commodity capital. This must be moved through financial networks based on banks, stockmarkets or commodity exchanges but does not require the relatively complex and stable sets of relationships associated with productive capital. Above all, it does not require the elaborate social and political systems within which accumulation of surplus value from human labour is accomplished. This helps to explain why a world economy which, at one level, is integrated by movements of money, becomes increasingly prone to destabilisation. It also explains the glaring contradictions associated with general movements of capital: how at one level such movements may prompt integration but at another level may have the effect of intensifying unevenness within the world system.

Financial capital: Even orthodox economists have recently become alarmed by the disproportion between what they call the 'paper' economy—debt—and 'fundamentals' such as growth in output. Drucker warns, 'Ninety percent or more of the transnational economy's financial transactions do not serve what economists would call an economic function'.[63] And Cerny comments that 'the financial economy calls the tune for the real economy'.[64] The suggestion that capital is not unitary has implications for the whole notion that increased flows of finance have been fundamental to the making of a globalised world.[65] It is especially relevant when we consider the place of Third World economies within the wider system.

Movements of capital in the form of money and of commodities have increased greatly in volume and speed over the past 30 years. Axford sums up the approach of many theorists by depicting this development as 'the most unequivocal indicator of the globalisation of economic affairs'.[66] In 1976 borrowing on international capital markets amounted to $96.6 billion; by 1993 the figure had reached $818.6 billion.[67] In addition, during the 1980s, markets in 'derivatives', speculation on interest rates and exchange rates, increased from a few hundred billion dollars annually to some $8,500 billion.[68] By 1995 the daily volume of business on the world's currency markets had reached $1,500 billion—a figure which exceeded the annual gross domestic product of all but three of the world's economies.[69]

Stopford and Strange describe the new environment in which these huge volumes of capital have become increasingly mobile:

Instead of a system of national financial systems linked by a few operators buying and selling credit across the exchanges, we now have a global system, in which national markets, physically separate, function as if they were all in the same place. The balance has shifted from a financial structure which was predominantly state based with some transnational links, to a predominantly global system in which some residual local differences in markets, institutions and regulations persist as vestiges of a bygone age.[70]

The new system, it is argued, has been made possible by rapid advances in communications technology. The *Financial Times* has observed that, because of these, banking 'is rapidly becoming indifferent to the constraints of time, place and currency'.[71] Changes in means of data transfer are often viewed as the defining expression of financial globality—a world 'wired' for integration between its banking centres is depicted as one already unified. It is in this context that Waters concludes, 'Elimination of space has accomplished the conquest of time'.[72] Such a notion of integration through financial flows has been a primary influence on theories of globalisation. In a revealing remark, Cerny suggests that today 'the world order follows the financial order'.[73]

These comments reflect the conviction of many globalisation theorists that world integration is a product of the autonomous functioning of modern technologies. In a typical observation, Gray notes, 'We are not the masters of the technologies that drive the global economy: they condition us in many ways we have not begun to understand'.[74] On this view, it is the power of digital systems that makes for integration of world finance. Such an approach offers no hint of why such means have been mobilised; in particular it ignores the initiatives taken by leading financial institutions to put new technologies to the service of profit.

In the 1970s many banks attempted to counter the problem of holding funds which were 'idle' due to recession in the West by lending to Third World countries. This was an effort to counter one manifestation of a general problem—the systemic tendency of the rate of profit to decline. It ended in near disaster, as Mexico defaulted, prompting the IMF to step in and rescue its financial institutions.[75] Banks were compelled to look elsewhere for means of maximising profit and there was a general turn towards 'securitisation'—selling shares, options and other forms of marketable 'paper' (including government debt) on stockmarkets worldwide. As banks moved more fully into these activities they pressed into service the technologies of communication which were just becoming available: integrated systems of computers, telephone lines, TV, and satellite links which allowed almost instantaneous transfers of funds, quick speculative gambits and rapid profit taking.[76]

The capacity to switch money at speed through global networks did not mean that the *relationships* mediated by money changed, however. Despite an appearance of 'indifference' to place, the mass of transactions were conducted within and between traditional financial centres such as New York, London and Tokyo. Even by the late 1980s over half of all 'stateless' currency—known as the Eurodollar—circulated within the US, principally among New York institutions that had dominated the money markets for decades.[77] And although penetration of finance capital into the Third World is now much deeper than hitherto, today's 'emerging markets' are often dominated by institutions which are direct descendants of banks and finance houses of the colonial era.

At the same time, large volumes of capital have been moved through new banking centres in the Third World, especially in East Asia and South East Asia, and globally organised speculative activities now affect profoundly many African, Asian and Latin American economies. Again, this is not an entirely novel development: during the colonial era bankers played a leading role in advancing European economic penetration of the Third World. In the post-colonial period many independent states then introduced controls, providing some insulation from capital movements in the wider market. But these measures were in turn reversed during the drive for deregulation which from the 1980s exposed such countries to more powerful flows of finance and to voracious profit seeking.

By the 1990s many countries which had been closed to international speculative activities were appearing on 'emerging markets' listings. In 1994 *Emerging Markets Investor* magazine detailed 51 emerging capital markets in which securities could be traded; it also commented that 'many of the markets currently inaccessible can be expected to open up before long'.[78] Within such markets all manner of institutions have been at work: in Egypt, for example, in 1995 only a handful of international financial operators were active; by 1997 some 714 foreign mutual funds had entered the local market, even though by world standards it traded a tiny volume of stocks.[79]

Although external financial involvement in many countries may be modest on the world scale, it may be very significant in the local context. This becomes apparent as the level of exposure to financial flows is increased, especially when Third World countries open stock exchanges or other markets on which a range of securities can be sold. Transnational movements of finance do not operate through the evenly integrated 24 hour global marketplace depicted in globalisation theory but through a series of interlinked networks—what management consultants McKinsey call 'distinct world markets for each type of instrument...depending closely on the complex nature of the risks which determine the price of each instrument in different countries'.[80] Markets in countries as diverse and physically distant as Bangladesh, Columbia, Ghana, Kenya, Pakistan, Peru and Vietnam have been drawn into these networks of speculative activity focused on short term profit taking. The result has been greatly increased vulnerability to speculators who make finely calculated judgements about each financial gambit, moving immense volumes of capital against local currencies and tradeable securities.

In 1997 the Malaysian ringitt and Thai baht dropped precipitately after evidence of local vulnerabilities produced huge outflows of money. Neighbouring states such as Vietnam and the Philippines, which were less exposed to the international markets but well integrated into the regional economy, also experienced steep falls in the value of their currencies and turmoil on their stockmarkets. There was a flood of money out of the region, mainly to secure 'home bases' in Europe, the US or Japan.[81]

Such is the fragility of many Third World currencies and local markets that specific local collapses can spread rapidly through financial networks, producing a 'contagion' effect. In August 1998 financial crisis in Russia prompted a collapse which the *Financial Times* said would cause developing markets in general to 'disappear into a black hole'— Third World currencies and stocks having become 'so much nuclear waste'.[82] Domestic interest rates in Brazil promptly rose to almost 50 percent and over a period of two weeks the Brazilian government spent $15 billion of its $67 billion foreign exchange reserves propping up its currency, the real.[83]

There can be no doubt that transnationalisation of world finance has had a profound effect, most importantly in generalising crisis. Thus events in South East Asia and Russia have not just weakened currencies in Latin America but through the 'domino effect' they threaten to subvert whole financial systems. In August 1998 the *Financial Times* warned that 'Latin America is on the brink':

> The Asian crisis, having swept through Russia, is now engulfing the continent. Its biggest economy, Brazil, is fighting to avoid a currency collapse or a debt moratorium. If it is forced into either, the next biggest economies, Argentina and Russia, would well follow suit...the economic reforms that opened up [Latin America] to the world market after a violent and inflationary decade will be at risk and so could the 'Washington consensus', the idea that economic modernisation is best performed by liberalising goods and capital markets.[84]

While predatory activity across the world has intensified, longer term involvement of major banks with the Third World has greatly diminished.[85] Lending has been directed to a small number of countries, notably to those in East Asia dubbed the 'Dragon' economies, which were said to be following the example of the East Asian Tigers and transforming themselves into industrialised states organised on uninhibited free market principles. In the first half of 1998 alone, international banks lent \$32 billion to countries in Asia, overwhelmingly to those in East and South Asia which were already showing what the *Financial Times* called (with some understatement) 'signs of strain'.[86] Speculative lending to Thailand, for example, had proved a key factor in precipitating a general economic collapse in 1997.[87] Meanwhile, less favoured economies elsewhere have become more dependent upon government borrowing, and upon programmes organised by the World Bank and the International Monetary Fund which continue to impose conditions in line with neo-liberal principles of deregulation, further emphasising local vulnerabilities.

'Free trade': The level of world integration through trade is much less pronounced than in the area of finance. It is true that during the long boom world trade grew very rapidly but growth rates have since slowed.[88] More important, trade is increasingly organised on a pattern at odds with the globalist notion of world integration.

In globalisation theory, deregulation is identified as the main means of achieving a free trade network in which commodities flow across old protective regimes. But developments among the world's dominant economies are not towards an open market model but towards regional links and trade agreements. Judis comments of the North American Free Trade Agreement (NAFTA) of 1992:

> *NAFTA is not really about global free trade. It does remove trade and investment barriers among the United States, Canada and Mexico, but it retains and erects (in the form of 'rules of origin') barriers between the three countries and the rest of the world.*
>
> *Appearances aside, NAFTA is a prudent step towards creating a regional trading bloc that would withstand the devolution of Western Europe and Asia into rival blocs. The treaty's free trade proponents would never admit this, but NAFTA's underlying thrust is toward managed trade and investment.*[89]

The notion that formation of such blocs represents a genuine alliance of national capitals must also be questioned. In the case of NAFTA, for example, regionalisation has been driven most strongly by US producers' desire to gain direct access to the Mexican market. During the late 1980s US exports to Mexico rose rapidly: Kegley and Wittkopf assert that 'NAFTA was written to accelerate this growth'.[90] Similarly, consolidation of the European Union (EU) should be understood in the context of the relative strengths of national states in the region. As Milward has argued in *The European Rescue of the Nation State*, Europeanisation is intimately associated with the dynamics of the most powerful of the regional economies, that of Germany.[91]

Rather than being integrated simply by trade flows, the global environment is also one of new blocs, each dominated by one or more of the major economic powers of North America, Europe and East Asia—what Sandholz calls 'regional neo-mercantilism'.[92] In the same vein *The Economist* challenges the idea of unstructured global interaction, commenting that 'the big trend in the world economy is towards "regionalism" and the reassertion of regional geography'.[93] Such blocs by definition exclude the mass of states of the Third World, viewed by the regional alliances as their arena for economic competition. The exceptions, such as Mexico in the NAFTA group, are left weaker as their notional independence is diminished. Even conservative accounts of the world order confirm this development. As Philips and Tucker comment, 'For the developing countries, the prospect of a world divided into separate regional centres is disconcerting. It leaves too many countries out of the system altogether, and even those it encompasses are left relatively weak as their bargaining power is divided'.[94]

Third World countries now occupy a more marginal position in world trade. In 1962 the share of 'industrial' countries was 63.6 percent and of 'non-industrial' countries 24.1 percent. By 1990 the figures were 71.9 percent and 20 percent respectively.[95] These figures place the four Asian Tigers in the 'non-industrial' group. If the four, which together have a quarter of the 'non-industrial' world's trade, are reallocated to the 'industrial' group, the figures reveal an even starker difference: 76.5 percent of world trade among 'industrial' countries and 16.5 percent of trade among the 'non-industrial' countries of the Third World. The picture is one of greatly increased asymmetry; notions of simple world integration once more seem implausible.

Productive capital and foreign direct investment: In the early 1970s, after 25 years of sustained growth through the 'long boom', international production seemed to be playing a new role in integrating the world economy. Exchange of manufactured goods became the most dynamic sector of world trade; at the same time, the internationalisation of manufacturing itself seemed to be breaking down barriers between national states. Harris noted, 'The great boom thus tended to wash away what hitherto had been seen as the clear national identification of production'.[96] Multinational companies (MNCs) were seen as the main agents of this process. Even by the early 1960s their combined sales were estimated at almost 20 percent of world output of goods and services and economists were beginning to depict a novel global development.[97] In fact MNCs had existed since at least the 19th century and their mode of operation was not new. What was unexpected was the speed of their growth and the contrast this presented with the preceding period during which national states and state capital had dominated the world economy.

By the early 1990s the largest 300 MNCs accounted for 70 percent of foreign direct investment (FDI) and 25 percent of the world's capital.[98] Most MNCs were engaged in extraction, processing or manufacture, the key sectors being petrochemicals, automobiles, consumer electronics, tyres, pharmaceuticals, tobacco and foodstuffs. They operated enterprises which required long term investment and demanded sophisticated local infrastructures. Most important, they employed tens of millions of workers in productive activities: that is, the exploitative relationships involved resulted directly in profit for the owners of capital. This places MNC activity in an altogether different category from other perceived globalising activities, notably that of finance, where, as Hoogvelt comments, profits 'are based on *fictitious* capital formation, namely on debt and exponential debt creation'.[99]

Even the repeated world recessions of the 1970s and 1980s, which deeply affected growth of trade, did not halt the process of restructuring. This can be seen in the rapid growth of FDI. Hirst and Thompson note that during the 1980s FDI grew almost four times faster than world merchandise trade, a development which these two writers—who are in general sceptical of the globalisation thesis—see as 'a very basic change in the nature of the international economy'.[100]

Chris Harman observes that much of the credibility of the 'globalisation' orthodoxy depends upon perceptions of MNC activity: 'It enables the orthodoxy to paint a picture of capital flowing evenly across the face of the earth, ceaselessly shifting from one spot to another in search of lower wages and higher profits, with a tendency towards the sprinkling of production facilities uniformly across all five continents'.[101] What is most striking about global investment, however, is that it too reveals a pattern of increasingly *uneven* development. On figures collected by Hoogvelt, until 1960 the Third World received about 50 percent of total world investment; by 1974 this had fallen to 25 percent; by 1988 it had fallen to 16.9 percent.[102] Thus during the colonial period, Africa, Asia and Latin America had been important target zones for investment; as the volume of total investment worldwide increased, these continents became less significant. FDI involves a much smaller proportion of investment. It grew significantly during the 1980s and especially in the 1990s, when the increase averaged 12 percent a year, almost double the increase in growth of total world exports.[103] By 1996 some 37 percent of total FDI was going to developing countries[104]—a statistic that has led many globalisers to conclude that FDI is widely dispersed. In fact, such capital entered only a handful of economies. The World Bank recently confirmed that between 1990 and 1995 just nine of the 147 'developing' countries received 90 percent of all such flows, the most favoured being China, Singapore, Malaysia, Thailand and Brazil.[105]

TEN TOP DEVELOPING COUNTRIES FOR INFLOW OF FDI
1981-1992 (US$ MILLION)

	1981	1986	1989	1992
China	—	1,875	3,393	11,156
Singapore	1,660	1,710	2,773	5,635
Mexico	2,835	1,523	3,037	5,366
Malaysia	1,265	489	1,668	4,469
Brazil	2,520	—	1,267	1,454
Hong Kong	1,088	996	1,076	1,918
Argentina	837	574	—	4,179
Thailand	—	—	1,775	2,116
Egypt	753	1,217	1,250	—
Taiwan	—	326	1,604	—

Percentage share of ten top countries in total inflows to developing countries:

| 81 | 70 | 72 | 76 |

[Source: UNCTAD]

Hirst and Thompson have correlated FDI with world population structure. They estimate that, even when major population centres such as coastal China are included in the recipient category, countries containing just 28 percent of the world's population receive 91.5 percent of the FDI.[106] They comment, 'In other words nearly two thirds of the world is virtually written off the map as far as any benefits from this form of investment are concerned'.[107]

This asymmetric pattern is consistent with the regionalisation of FDI within economies of the West. Ruigrok and van Tulder show that almost all MNCs invest more in one country than in any other: that in effect they operate from a clearly established 'home base' or within a distinct region close to the national point of origin.[108] This is also consistent with patterns of world trade which show regional networks and the consolidation of trading blocs. Kiely concludes that 'evidence points to the maintenance, and indeed the *intensification* of uneven development in the global economy'.[109]

Home base: In a recent critique of globalisation theory, Chris Harman comments, 'It is very easy for firms which trade internationally to move money internationally. But moving money is not the same thing as moving productive capital.' He goes on:

> *Productive capital is made up of factories and machinery, mines, docks, offices and so on. These take years to build up and cannot be simply picked up and carted away... Productive capital simply cannot be footloose.*[110]

Kiely makes a similar point, that 'capital faces a number of sunk costs, which constitute significant barriers to exit'.[111] He quotes Wade: '[Such costs] include initial start up costs, the costs of learning over time about a particular environment, and the costs of building, reputation, gaining acceptance among government, employees and other firms regarding their reliability as producers, employers, and suppliers in each market.[112]

Labour costs are only one factor in decisions about location made by MNCs. Corporate managers routinely summon up the idea of a globalised labour market in which their workforce must be prepared to accept the discipline imposed by market conditions. But the idea of global portability of jobs is false. The most that can be said is that in some labour intensive industries such as clothing, textiles and electronic assembly, fixed costs are lower than in most other sectors and capital is somewhat more mobile. Korzeniewicz has shown, by analysing the activities of footwear manufacturer Nike in East Asia, that companies must balance the gain in lower wages against a host of other factors. He comments, 'The advantages of lower labour costs in the developing manufacturing areas [have] to be weighed against disadvantages in production flexibility, quality, raw material sourcing and transportation'.[113] In many cases, relatively high wage locations prove more desirable.

These considerations do not mean that companies remain wholly within the national state of origin. But even in the late 1990s relatively few have moved outside their *regional* bases, where they can rely on well established industrial links and infrastructures. Ruigrok and van Tulder conclude that, under these circumstances, 'neither individual firms nor states but industrial complexes constitute the centre of gravity of the international restructuring race'.[114] Three such complexes dominate the world economy: North America, Europe and Japan. The rest of the world contributes only 19 percent of the sum of manufacturing exports and of this total two thirds comes from the Tiger economies, plus coastal China.[115] There is no sign elsewhere of the development of major industrial complexes which might relocate productive capital on a substantial scale. It is on this basis that Ruigrok and van Tulder argue that what is usually called 'globalisation' would be better described as 'triadisation'.[116]

In this context structures congenial to long term investment of capital are of immense importance. When MNCs do invest outside regions of origin the character of the local state is a critical factor and nation states perceived as stable, with well-integrated infrastructures and mechanisms of social and political control, are highly favoured. As Kiely observes, the pattern of FDI worldwide takes place 'because of, and not despite the state'.[117] There is a corollary: those states without attributes deemed necessary by MNCs are treated with suspicion and few Third World states are considered for serious long term investment. Capitalism is not using the Third World in general as a site for intensified exploitation, it is marginalising it.

Globalisation and development

NICs—road closed: Globalisation theory is not a description of a much changed world. Rather it is the imposition of neo-liberal economic principles upon the reality of an unequal and disordered system: the world as contemporary bourgeois theory wishes it to be.

It is certainly true that the internationalisation of capital has accelerated over the past 30 years. But within this process two developments have taken the system in a direction different from that envisaged by the globalisers. First, a key response to the fall in the rate of profit has been increased speculative activity and a huge growth in financial markets. This has not complemented the growth of productive capital at a global level but has diverted investible funds from it, making less likely the emergence of new centres of capital accumulation. A second development involves decisions taken by MNCs to develop manufacturing on a regional, rather than a 'global' basis. Emergence of the 'triad' of investment zones has concentrated more and more of productive capital among networks of advanced economies. These networks are connected to Third World economies but are not active agents of the latters' development; on the contrary, their consolidation is a vote of 'no confidence' in the Third World. Declining rates of productive investment have left most such economies weak and vulnerable to the currents, eddies and tidal waves created by global speculators. The two tendencies have a combined effect of greatly increasing the development 'gap' between the 'triad' and the NICs, and 'the rest'. They intensify the unevenness of the world system, relegating to the also-rans even those states in which there were once hopes of modest advance.

These changes mean that the vision of advance towards NIC status is an illusion. In the mid-1980s Nigel Harris argued that the experience of the NICs would become *more* general. The dispersal of capital world-wide would certainly involve more and more economies, he argued: 'Once the internationalised core was created, the effects spread out-wards, involving increased numbers of less developed countries, so that there are new newly industrialising countries—it is a continuing process. It seems inconceivable that the general trend could now be reversed'.[118]

But the trend *has* been reversed. What now seems inconceivable is that even among the more stable countries of Africa, Asia and Latin America there might emerge states able to follow the paths of Korea or Taiwan, which over a generation from the 1940s changed radically, becoming substantial (if junior) industrial capitalisms. Callinicos's criti-cisms of Harris in this journal in 1987 have proved substantially correct. Emergence of new NICs, Callinicos suggested, would 'depend heavily upon international conditions reflecting largely the state of the advanced economies' and would be 'limited by the ways in which Western capital-ists, still the dominant force in the system, respond to the fall in the world rate of profit'.[119]

In effect, capitalism has closed the NIC option for the forseeable future. Its ideologues nonetheless maintain a double fiction: that indus-trialisation *can* be achieved and that the appropriate strategy is based upon a specific model of the free market NIC. As recently as 1997, one leading US bank published lists of Tigers, Near-Tigers and Tiger Cubs, encouraging Third World governments to believe that they could join the developing elite.[120] Many ruling classes remain susceptible to the vision of progress within a 'globalised' world, in which pursuit of free market policies on the Tiger model will bring developmental rewards. In fact, from the 1940s, regimes in the East Asian NICs had followed a state cap-italist path to industrialisation and represent specific and probably unrepeatable cases of rapid capital accumulation in the Third World. As Harris argued, 'Before the four existed, it had been necessary to invent them in order to justify [neo-liberal theories]; and after they expanded, not a little invention went into rendering the facts of their performance consistent with the postulates of the free market'.[121]

Especially misleading is the notion that in cases of the most rapid advance, notably Korea, the local state withdrew from direct intervention in economic affairs. On the contrary, the state was (and remains) central: as one account of Korea notes, 'No state outside the Socialist bloc came anywhere near this measure of control over the state's investible resources'.[122] The fiction of Korean development has nonetheless been incorporated into theories of globalisation to make an apparently seamless argument for free market strategy. Institutions such as the World Bank and the IMF continue to embellish the myth while using control over funds to induce Third World governments to move away from protectionism, state ownership and market controls.

Such 'liberalisation' was pioneered in the mid-1970s by the Sadat regime in Egypt through its *infitah* ('opening') policy. The regime immediately enriched itself and its supporters through commission agencies, import-export scams, and speculation in property and finance. Within a few years a 'Sadat class' of *nouveaux riches* had been accommodated by the ruling senior bureaucrats and army officers of the earlier nationalist period. Hinnebusch describes the outcome:

> *The new prosperity widened and solidified the regime's support among those who got the lion's share of the benefits, the bourgeoisie. Revitalisation of the private sector created powerful interests with a stake in the regime. Contractors, real estate speculators, and merchants flourished on the economic boom; importers, partners and agents of foreign firms, tourist operators, lawyers and middle men who helped investors against bureaucratic tangles, thrived on the cuts they took from resource inflow... On the other hand, the lower middle and lower classes bore the main costs of infitah while reaping the fewest benefits... The explosion of conspicuous consumption at the top fed a growing perception that class gaps were widening, the rich getting rich and the poor poorer.[123]*

Twenty five years after the initiation of *infitah* President Mubarak still talks of creating a 'Tiger on the Nile' but sustained industrial growth on the NIC model remains a distant prospect. The story has been repeated in scores of states worldwide, as regimes with roots in an earlier era of state-led development have embraced neo-liberalism and launched the inevitable attacks upon living standards, social welfare and upon workers' and peasants' rights.

The African crisis: In many poor countries the aim of development policy has been less ambitious—simply to halt economic decline. In 1991 the UN secretary general commented that Africa was heading for 'an unrelenting crisis of tragic proportions'.[124] But for African states the solution has been the same as for aspiring industrialisers—the implementation of 'adjustment' programmes which aim to create conditions congenial to private capital accumulation.[125] The outcome has been to intensify crisis: in agricultural production, industrial output, increased deforestation and desertification, rising food imports, declining terms of trade and capital flight. Sandbrook comments, 'If it were not for the unenumerated and unregulated informal or parallel economy, life [for the masses] would be more even desperate'.[126]

The more compliant have been local regimes, the more seriously they have been affected. In 1990 Zimbabwe was ranked as a 'middle income' country by the World Bank, above Indonesia, the Philippines and other states aspiring to rapid advance.[127] With mineral wealth and a relatively sophisticated agricultural sector it was expected to progress much faster than other African countries. While opposing IMF 'adjustment' programmes rhetorically, the Mugabe regime had implemented them, fulfilling requirements for aid and development assistance. But during the mid-1990s world prices for Zimbabwe's main exports, tobacco and gold, fell sharply and investors began to withdraw. In November 1997 there was a run on the local currency and a collapse in the Harare stockmarket. Food prices soared and were given a further upward push when, under pressure from the World Bank and IMF, the Zimbabwean regime increased the cost of the main staple, maize, by 24 percent.[128] Following strikes and demonstrations against the increases there was a further collapse as the Zimbabwean dollar—formerly regarded as one of the best speculative investments in Africa—halved in value against the US dollar. One report commented that in a few months the country had gone from being one of Africa's top performers—'about to achieve sustained growth and prosperity'—to 'economic disaster'.[129]

Zimbabwe suffers from the increased vulnerability which affects all economies 'opened' to the world system. As a corollary, states which have been somewhat less compliant with the IMF, or less effective in 'opening', have been punished less heavily. After the collapse of world markets in September 1998 one investment manager in London commented, 'As liquidity has drained out of the emerging markets, countries with relatively little foreign participation and generally illiquid markets have suffered the least...minor markets...seem to be unaffected by turmoil elsewhere'.[130] While countries such as Somalia, Liberia, Sierra Leone, Sudan, Haiti and Afghanistan are dismissed as 'basket cases' and written out of the development script, others are penalised for having played their allocated role.

At the same time, these very vulnerable countries are being revisited by the problem of debt. This has often been viewed as a problem of the 1970s and early 1980s which receded when commercial banks reduced lending. But everywhere except Latin America (scene of the earlier debt crisis) debts to Western governments and multilateral creditors have continued to mount. By the late 1980s the volume of debt was increasing massively: in 1990 the total stock of debt owed by developing countries was $1.4 trillion; by 1997 it was $2.17 trillion.[131] In Africa by 1997 debt stood at $370 for every person in the continent and dwarfed the annual production of many states.[132] In 1994 Mozambique's debt amounted to

450 percent of its GNP, that of Congo was 454 percent of GNP, and of the Ivory Coast 339 percent of GNP.[133] Scores of countries were similarly entrapped. Despite the increase in FDI to some developing economies, Western banks and governments now receive more in interest on debt from the Third World than the MNCs extract in profit—a reversal of the situation in the 1970s.[134] In 1998 Third World countries paid Western creditors $717 million in debt service every day.[135]

AFRICAN DEBT 1994—SELECTED STATES

	Total debt (US$ billion)	Debt as % of GNP
Congo	5.3	454
Mozambique	5.5	450
Guinea-Bissau	0.8	340
Ivory Coast	18.5	339
Angola	11.2	275
Dem Rep of Congo	12.3	232
Tanzania	7.4	230
Madagascar	4.1	225
Zambia	6.6	204
Sierra Leone	1.4	187
Malawi	2.0	160
Togo	1.5	157

[Source: World Bank, *World Development Report 1996*]

PROFIT AND INTEREST: OUTFLOWS FROM THE THIRD WORLD (US$ BILLION)

	1970	1980	1990	1994
Interest	2.4	35.1	59.4	64.5
Profit	6.5	24.0	17.8	25.4

[Source: World Bank]

With commodity prices falling, and the trade liberalisation of the Uruguay Round of negotiations on tariffs further penalising Third World economies, such countries might have expected relaxation of payment conditions. But in 1998 the US stalled on its Highly Indebted Poor

Countries initiative (HIPC). Countries such as Tanzania, which was told to wait until 2002 to qualify for promised 'debt relief' under HIPC, face crushing burdens. According to one aid agency, the country's debt is rising so rapidly that development projects are hardly feasible. A Christian Aid official illustrates a problem which is causing anxiety to even the most conservative aid bodies: rigorous enforcement of repayments by the World Bank for borrowing on projects which the institution designed and which could never have achieved its own target results. According to Andrew Simms, 'Tanzania is paying for the World Bank's own mistakes. The money is simply going round in circles.' He adds:

> There's one project in Tanzania for which we borrowed about $9 million. In 1979, that was equal to about 149 million [Tanzanian] shillings. So far we have repaid about $900,000 but that is now equivalent to 590 million shillings. In local currency terms we have already repaid the debt several times. But it just goes up and up.[136]

What seems incomprehensible to aid officials is that Tanzania has implemented IMF adjustment programmes, as instructed, since the mid-1980s. Among its 'liberalisation' measures, the government has repeatedly devalued the local currency, so that by 1998 the shilling was at 1,500 percent less than its international value in 1985. The government now spends $8 for every Tanzanian to service its external debt while it spends just $3 annually per person on health.[137] More than 50 percent of the population lives below the poverty line.

These stark problems have not prevented US strategists restating the global masterplan in blunt terms. In 1997 the State Department sent a senior trade official to tell an African summit meeting: 'The core premises of our plan are that those nations willing and able to pursue the most aggressive growth oriented economic policies—principally by opening their economies to the world marketplace—are the ones most likely to be the engines of growth on the continent'.[138]

Global inequality

End of the 'Third World'? The notion of a 'Third World' has never been closely defined. As deployed by radical nationalists in the 1950s it was meant to indicate a state directed development path independent of Western capitalism and of Eastern state capitalism. This homogenised a vast range of countries; it also concealed class relations within them and the common interests between their rulers and those of the 'First' and 'Second' worlds. As such it obscured the workings of capitalism. Since the 1970s the main use of the term has been as a shorthand to indicate the

gulf between a minority of rich countries and the majority of poor countries of Africa, Asia and Latin America. As an expression of
contemporary world inequalities it may then be more significant than
hitherto—for such inequalities have become far more pronounced. In
addition, it is a useful corrective to globalist babble with its imagined
universe of happy consumers.

In globalisation theory the notion of a Third World is rendered meaningless, for the inequalities it implies are said to be disappearing beneath
worldwide capital flows. This is Nigel Harris's position in *The End of the
Third World*, published in 1986, in which he argued that a strong tendency
to distribution of manufacturing across the globe was transforming relations between rich and poor countries. But neither the notion of a
globalised world, nor that of a system divided between First and Third
worlds (or North and South) are appropriate ways of depicting world capitalism. The system is best seen as a series of unevenly developed
economic and political structures, including nation states and regions,
within which capital is mobilised in the constant search for profit.

This system is structured by class. It is true that national economies
stand in a hierarchy, with Western capitalist states at the head and a long
tail of Third World countries. But this structure depends upon the maintenance of class relations which cross-cut the hierarchy, tying minorities
of the wealthy and powerful in Africa, Asia and Latin America to the
centres of world power. The emergence of the NICs in the 1950s and
1960s represented the efforts of capital in a handful of countries to
exploit local working classes with enough success to consolidate a
stronger position *vis à vis* other capitals and in effect to climb the hierarchy. The ruling class of South Korea, for example, only accomplished
this under uniquely favourable circumstances and as *part* of the system
of world exploitation. In doing so, it both co-operated closely with the
centres of power *and* developed its own distinct interests at the expense
of the Korean working class.

The increased internationalisation of capital has made for closer relationships between the subordinate ruling classes of Africa, Asia and
Latin America, and the centres of world power. The former have largely
abandoned state led development policies in favour of neo-liberal formulas drawn up in Washington, Tokyo and London, which they believe
to be beneficial to their interests. But as the outcome of such policies
becomes clearer, problems which have always attended co-operation
among capitalists (Marx's 'band of warring brothers') have started to re-
emerge. These have affected the new trading blocs, global agreements,
and local economies and states. There have been a number of preliminary tremors: the US has been unable to drive through its World Trade
Agreement; the US and the EU have fallen out over tariffs; and Middle

Eastern states promised a new trade deal with the EU have begun to complain bitterly about broken promises. In August 1998 the *Financial Times* warned of a 'severe protectionist backlash' in the US which could intensify as businesses dived for cover under the protection of the national state.[139] But the real shock has come with repeated currency meltdowns and generalised crisis in South East Asia. This has brought the whole economic orthodoxy into question. Former free market fanatic Mahathir Mohamad of Malaysia has blamed 'foreign capital' and 'speculators' for his difficulties and attempted a move towards autarkic local solutions by banning sales of the ringgit and organising state buyouts of non-performing loans and assets of banks—heresies among his one time friends of the neo-liberal establishment. US financier George Soros—a totemic figure for ideologues of globalisation—has attacked Mahathir as 'a menace to his own country'.[140]

Soros is also in a state of panic, however. To the surprise of the neo-liberals, he has been a leading figure in calling for new structures for supervision of the global market: in effect, he wishes for a global state which will guarantee his own worldwide search for speculative gain. Increasingly perplexed by the instabilities of the world system, he has become a new prophet of global doom, suggesting, 'The collapse of the global marketplace would be a traumatic event with unimaginable consequences. Yet I find it easier to imagine than continuation of the present regime'.[141] Leading US economist Paul Krugman has argued that only extensive capital controls can rescue the Asian economies and that urgent action is needed. These formulas are viewed with alarm by fundamentalist neo-liberals. For *The Economist* they constitute 'a worrying backlash against free markets'.[142] Third World countries must go on bending to 'market discipline', argues the magazine—only then will they be rewarded with prosperity 'for decades to come'.[143] Increasingly, speculators, industrialists, governments and economic journalists have turned on one another. As one US economist observed, 'The International Monetary Fund blames the national governments, the national governments blame the outsiders, and the populations blame some combination of the two'.[144]

Crisis and conflict: World crisis has intensified conflict at every level of the system. While governments and global institutions attempt to allocate blame, much more costly conflict takes place within and between national states, especially in the Third World. This often has its roots in divisions built into the colonial state by occupying powers, a problem exacerbated by liberalisation policy and by deepening systemic crisis. Regimes under pressure from below may fragment and contending factions attempt to mobilise support on a regional, religious or ethnic basis. The state may implode and basic infrastructure for supply of food or of healthcare may break up, causing vast numbers of people to flee, creating what Zolberg has called 'the exit from the state'.[145] Just such a situation occurred in the Horn of Africa in the early 1990s and in West Africa in the mid-1990s, when millions of people in Liberia and Sierra Leone were displaced. Under these circumstances external powers may attempt to intervene, as in Somalia, which the US invaded in an unsuccessful attempt to re-establish centralised authority—an interesting example of reassertion of structures of the nation state in a 'globalised' era.

Even in less marginal regions economic crisis may produce sudden mass population movements. One response of regimes in South East Asia to the 'meltdown' of 1997 was to target migrant labour. At least 2.5 million workers in Thailand and Malaysia, and 270,000 in South Korea, were identified as a threat to national security. Some were incarcerated and many were deported, especially to Indonesia, Burma and Bangladesh.[146] Attempts by regimes to mobilise national sentiments can also spiral into sudden regional conflicts. Just such a scenario emerged in mid-1998 in the Horn of Africa, where Eritrea and Ethiopia began an armed conflict, ostensibly over territory but which could only be under-stood in the context of impacts of world crisis upon two very weak economies in which rulers were ready to mobilise all means to ensure their survival.

Struggles from below: The desire within the capitalist class for more solid political structures within the global system is intimately linked to immense pressures from below. Since the deepening of world crisis in the 1970s every region of the Third World has seen the emergence of mass movements which have challenged local regimes and regional power structures. These have often taken the form of protests against IMF adjustment programmes. In 1974 the Egyptian regime was first to declare for liberalisation, launching Sadat's *infitah*. It was immediately confronted by widespread opposition and for three years Egyptian society was in turmoil as workers, peasants and the poor engaged in all manner of protests against reduced subsidies on food and fuel, rising prices and rents, and increased political repression. Workers were espe-cially prominent, launching the biggest strike wave since the independence struggles of the late 1940s. In January 1977, following further IMF-inspired cuts, there was a massive upheaval which com-bined nationwide strikes with demonstrations, riots and prolonged battles with the police and the army. In Cairo, wrote journalist David Hirst, a vast sea of humanity bore down upon the presidential palace:

The thwarted multitude became...a raging torrent, an uncontrollable force which...unleashed all their pent-up fury on targets which, for them, symbolised the yawning gap between the haves and the have-nots, the frivolity and corruption of the ruling class, the incompetence and blind insensitivity of the administration... It was a despairing protest against the unspeakable conditions in which they had to earn their daily bread.[147]

Tanks and artillery were mobilised against the movement but it required withdrawal of the price increases—what Hirst describes as an 'ignominious climbdown'—to save the regime. During the 1980s similar protests against IMF programmes affected states across the Middle East: Morocco, Tunisia, Jordan, Lebanon—and Algeria, where in 1988 a prolonged mass movement brought the regime to the brink of collapse. By the early 1990s such events were so widespread that media routinely referred to the 'IMF riot'. But throughout this period partisans of globalisation, with their visions of social harmony induced by the market, preferred to ignore the whole phenomenon of mass action. Meanwhile the Iranian Revolution of 1978-1979—a testimony to the impacts of uneven development and authoritarian rule which mobilised millions of people (and caused deep anxiety among Western states)—was explained away as a manifestation of Islamic perversity.

During the 1990s the pace of struggle has intensified, with an unprecedented wave of protests across Africa, notably in Zambia, Malawi, Nigeria, Kenya and Zimbabwe. These have often been linked specifically to IMF inspired adjustment programmes and their outcomes. In South East Asia the Tiger Cubs have been in turmoil. Suharto, viewed in the West as a model liberaliser, has been brought down by a movement of immense power. In Malaysia the masses have rediscovered a voice after years of repression by the Mahathir regime. The Tigers themselves are in deep crisis: in a recent analysis in the *Financial Times*, investors were warned that South Korea had strong trade unions capable of mounting mass resistance to rising unemployment and that President Kim Dae-jung might be removed.[148] Everywhere, rulers fear not only the 'contagion' of economic collapse but the spread of collective struggle— a 'domino effect' in which resistance is generalised across states and even continents.[149]

Although analysis of recent trends reveals that the spread of manufacturing industry outside the 'triad' networks has been exaggerated, the number of workers worldwide continues to grow. In 1980 in the Third World and former Eastern Bloc countries combined there were 285 million industrial workers (excluding those in the informal sector); by 1994 there were 407 million such workers.[150] The working class is not only more numerous but is in general better organised. This is most obvious in some of the newer NICs, where unions have grown with remarkable speed and, especially in South Korea and Taiwan, have proved a potent political force. In countries such as Brazil, India, Turkey and Egypt the working class is especially resilient: in the latter the latest wave of denationalisation measures has foundered on workers' refusal to accept erosion of benefits first granted in the 1950s. And in Africa the protests of the 1990s have been notable for the high level of engagement by organised workers, especially in South Africa, Kenya and Zimbabwe.

Millions of such workers and their families live under conditions which express precisely the character of combined and uneven development. As a leading Brazilian trade unionist has explained, 'Who lives in *favelas* [shanty-towns] today is the worker of the most sophisticated industries of the country, the worker at Volkswagen, of Philips, of Villares, Mercedes etc'.[151] Many such workers also retain ties to the land. In 1997 the Egyptian government attempted to dismantle the Nasserist land reforms of the 1950s. This 'liberalisation' of the rural economy, much favoured by the IMF, has implications for millions of peasant families and soon provoked a response as police enforcing eviction orders on tenant farmers were confronted by mass protests. There were also demonstrations in major industrial centres, notably in the Nile Delta city of Mehalla al-Kubra, where tens of thousands of textile workers whose families in neighbouring villages had a vital stake in the land, joined the protests. Alarmed by the prospect of rural resistance combined with mass strikes at the heart of the country's biggest industry, the regime quickly modified its plans.

Mainstream globalisation theory denies such human agency. If human beings feature at all in the globalist account it is passively, as consumers. A similar position is adopted in accounts by revisionists who wish to salvage the global paradigm, suggesting that at best it might be possible to restrain global forces. For pessimists such as Gray we are on the brink of a 'tragic epoch' in which the forces of anarchy threaten humanity and in which we must turn to the works of Hobbes and Malthus for explanations of our predicament.[152] We would do better to turn to Marx, whose understanding of the dynamics of capitalism both anticipated world crisis and offered a means to supercede its barbarism. Trotsky, too, saw the character of a growing world system and the emergence of a political collective capable of changing it. In 1905, explaining the emergence of societies such as Russia, marked by the process of combined and uneven development, he argued:

> Binding all countries together with its mode of production and its commerce, capitalism has converted the whole world into a single economic and political organism. Just as modern credit binds thousands of undertakings by invisible ties and gives to capital an incredible mobility which prevents many small bankruptcies but at the same time is the cause of the unprecedented sweep of

general economic crisis, so the whole economic and political effort of capital,
its world trade, its system of monstrous state debts, and the political groupings
of nations which draw all the forces of reaction into a kind of worldwide joint-
stock company, has not only resisted all individual political crises, but also
prepared the basis for a social crisis of unheard of dimensions.[153]

This crisis, Trotsky argued, had an international character, in which
local struggles necessarily had a wider impact. Revolutionary upheaval
in Russia, he insisted, must place on the agenda the question of world
change. A dozen years later the October Revolution had just this effect.
Almost 100 years later, with a vastly more developed global economy,
the crisis of capitalism is deep and systemic, the class capable of
bringing change is larger, more widely spread and showing every sign of
increased combativity. It remains, in Trotsky's words, 'the initiator of the
liquidation of world capitalism'.[154]

Notes

Thanks to Gary McFarlane for some valuable data, and to John Rees, Adrian Budd, John
Rose and Eli Povey for their comments on the article in draft.

1   M Waters, *Globalization* (London, 1995), p1.
2   L Elliott, *The Guardian*, 2 February 1998.
3   'The World in 1998', *The Economist*, Special Report, December 1997.
4   UNDP, *Human Development Report 1998* (New York, 1998).
5   C Caufield, *Masters of Illusion: The World Bank and the Poverty of Nations*
      (London, 1998), p332.
6   UNDP, op cit.
7   Ibid.
8   *The Independent*, 17 November 1998.
9   UNDP, op cit.
10   Ibid.
11   L Elliott and A Brummer, Special Report on the IMF, *The Guardian*, 3 July 1998.
12   *Financial Times*, 8 January 1998.
13   Quoted in *The Independent*, 10 February 1997.
14   W Keegan, 'Bankers Hold Out Against War On Slump', *The Observer*, 20
      September 1998.
15   Ibid.
16   M Nicholson, *International Relations* (Basingstoke, 1998), p65.
17   J Gray, *False Dawn* (London, 1998), p206.
18   Ibid, p64.
19   Ibid. Several revisions of globalisation dismiss early theorists as
      'hyperglobalisers' and as 'utopian' (see D Held, D Goldblatt, A McGrew, J
      Jerraton, 'The Globalization of Economic Activity', *New Political Economy*, vol
      2, no 2, July 1997). Gray also goes to pains to explain 'what globalisation is not',
      with the purpose of rescuing the idea from those he dubs 'extreme globalisers' (J
      Gray, ibid, p76).
20   The question of which theory of globalisation to address has also provoked debate
      among US academics associated with the *Monthly Review* journal. The exchanges
      reveal how disorienting are notions of globalisation which accept the globalisers'

terms of reference and their contention that a positive world integration has been accomplished. See the articles by Tabb, Du Boff and Herman, and Ellen Meiskins Wood in *Monthly Review*, June, July-August, and November 1997.

21   B Axford, *The Global System* (Cambridge, 1995), p94.
22   P Hirst and G Thompson, *Globalization in Question* (Cambridge, 1996), p195.
23   Ibid, p195. Globalisers appear to be unanimous in relation to the nation state, which is said to have been weakened or even rendered irrelevant by economic processes. Horsman and Marshall present a typical analysis, suggesting that, 'Effortless communications across boundaries undermines the nation state's control; increased mobility, and the increased willingness of people to migrate, undermine its cohesiveness. Business abhors borders and seeks to circumnavigate them... The nation state...is increasingly powerless to withstand these pressures.' Quoted in I Douglas, 'Globalisation and the End of the State?', in *New Political Economy* 2:1 (1997), p167.
24   A Hoogvelt, *Globalisation and the Post-Colonial World* (Basingstoke, 1997), p124.
25   N FitzGerald, 'Harnessing the Potential of Globalization for the Consumer and Citizen', *International Affairs*, vol 73, no 4, October 1997, p741.
26   Ibid.
27   N Harris, *The New Untouchables* (London, 1997), p228.
28   W I Robinson, 'Globalisation: Nine Theses for our Epoch', *Race and Class* 38:2 (1996), p28.
29   Ibid, p14.
30   Ibid, p13.
31   M Waters, op cit, p95.
32   Such a view might be seen as merely bizarre or as the 'utopian' vision of a few academics and corporate strategists if it were not one embraced in thousands of boardrooms. Evidence of the reality of world integration and of social harmonisation is seen in the emergence of new social categories such as the 'global teens' said to occupy a 'global space'—'a single pop-culture world, soaking up the same videos and music and providing a huge market for designer running shoes, T-shirts and jeans'. These new layers of consumers, whose tastes cross old political and cultural boundaries, are viewed as testimony to the global condition. So for FitzGerald of Unilever we now live in a 'world of diminishing borders, corporate responsibility, individualism and consumer power'. Its true benefits lie in the relations that can be established between business and consumer: in the new era, it is a matter of 'harnesssing the potential of globalization for the consumer and citizen' (N FitzGerald, op cit, p739).
33   UNDP, *Human Development Report 1997* (Oxford University Press, 1997).
34   Ibid.
35   Ibid.
36   Ibid.
37   Quoted in W I Robinson, op cit, p29.
38   Ibid.
39   *The Guardian*, 28 August 1997.
40   *The Guardian*, 17 October 1998.
41   Philippines President Joseph Estrada, reported in *The Guardian*, 14 October 1998.
42   *The Guardian*, ibid.
43   R Cox, 'Critical Political Economy', in B Hettne et al (eds), *International Political Economy: Understanding Global Disorder* (London, 1995), p41.
44   Reported in UNDP (1998), p30.
45   Ibid
46   Ibid.
47   Ibid.

48   R El-Ghonemy, *Affluence and Poverty in the Middle East* (London, 1998), p231.
49   K Marx and F Engels, 'The Communist Manifesto', in K Marx and F Engels, *Selected Works* (Moscow, 1962), pp34-35.
50   Ibid.
51   K Marx, 'The Future Results of the British Rule in India', in K Marx and F Engels, *On Colonialism* (Foreign Languages Publishing House), p84.
52   K Marx, 'The British Rule in India', in K Marx, *On Colonialism,* op cit, p39.
53   Ibid, p37.
54   Engels on the bourgeoisie in the German Revolution, in F Engels, 'Revolution and Counter-revolution in Germany', in K Marx and F Engels, *Selected Works,* op cit, vol 1, p300.
55   K Marx, 'The Future Results of the British Rule in India', op cit, p88.
56   Quoted in I Cummins, *Marx, Engels and the National Movements* (London, 1981), p147.
57   L Trotsky, 'Results and Prospects', in *The Permanent Revolution and Results and Prospects* (New York, 1969), p49.
58   Ibid, p51.
59   A Callinicos, 'Imperialism, Capitalism and the State Today', *International Socialism* 2:35 (1987), p108.
60   P Harrison, *Inside the Third World* (London, 1993), p350.
61   Ibid, p351.
62   C Harman, 'The State and Capitalism Today', *International Socialism* 2:51 (1991), p9.
63   Quoted in A Hoogvelt, op cit, p128.
64   P Cerny, 'The Political Economy of International Finance', *Finance and World Politics* (Edward Elgar, 1993), p18.
65   Much of the money in the new networks is associated with the circulation of money itself. What Strange calls 'casino capitalism' amounts to a huge increase in debt, especially private debt, and in secondary speculation against it. According to UNCTAD, during the 1980s the ratio of the size of international bank lending to the size of the world's total fixed investment (a measure of the 'real' economy) more than doubled. By 1992 world indebtedness exceeded even the total gross domestic product of the richest (OECD) countries.
66   B Axford, op cit, p107.
67   P Hirst and G Thompson, op cit, p40.
68   Ibid, p41.
69   From H Shutt, 'The Trouble with Capitalism', quoted in *The Independent*, 30 June 1998.
70   J Stopford and S Strange, *Rival States, Rival Firms* (Cambridge,1991), pp40-41.
71   D Harvey, *The Condition of Postmodernity* (Oxford, 1989), p161.
72   M Waters, op cit, p88.
73   P Cerny, op cit, p18.
74   J Gray, op cit, p206.
75   See P Green, 'Debt, the Banks and Latin America,' *International Socialism* 2:21 (1983).
76   Callinicos comments of this 'parasitism' that it reflected the continuing low rate of return in manufacturing industry: 'a consequence of the crisis of profitability which capitalism entered in the late 1960s and has still to escape' (A Callinicos, op cit, p92).
77   M Waters, op cit, p187.
78   *Emerging Markets Factbook* (London, 1994).
79   *Ahram Weekly* (Cairo), 23 April 1997.
80   Quoted in P Cerny, op cit, p68.

81 In a similar development in 1991 Iraq's invasion of Kuwait prompted a mass movement of money from Gulf banking centres such as Bahrain to accounts in London and New York. Billions of dollars moved overnight. See P Cerny, op cit, p69. During the Thai and Malaysian 'meltdowns' of 1997 the *Financial Times* reported large redemptions of Asian funds in the US, adding that events in South East Asia would prove a source of underlying support for the US market 'as investors flee to quality'. Such rapid movement of capital to traditional financial centres within dominant nation states speaks eloquently of the latters' continuing weight within the world system. See the *Financial Times*, 30 August 1997.

82 Richard Waters in the *Financial Times*, 29 August 1998.

83 *The Observer*, 13 September 1998.

84 *Financial Times*, 12 August 1998.

85 Lending by international banks in Africa, Asia and Latin America rose very rapidly in the 1970s; within a decade, however, the debt crisis and increased general instability had all but brought it to an end. By 1989 lending to Africa, Asia and Latin America was just 11 percent of the global total. (A Hoogvelt, op cit, p83). The earlier debts remained.

86 *Financial Times*, 5 January 1998.

87 See C Sparks, 'The Eye of the Storm', *International Socialism* 2:78 (1998).

88 During the 1960s it accelerated rapidly, reaching an annual increase of 9 percent by 1973 (P Hirst and G Thompson, op cit, pp21-22). By the mid-1990s the rate of growth was unchanged over the level attained a decade earlier (A Hoogvelt, op cit, p71).

89 C Kegley and E Wittkopf, *World Politics* (New York, 1995), p247.

90 Ibid, p247.

91 A Milward, *The European Rescue of the Nation State* (London, 1992), p134.

92 C Kegley and E Wittkopf, op cit, p247.

93 *The Economist*, 20 November 1993.

94 C Kegley and E Wittkopf, op cit, p265.

95 A Hoogvelt, op cit, p73.

96 N Harris, *The End of the Third World* (London, 1986), p58.

97 Ibid, p59.

98 M Waters, op cit, p76.

99 A Hoogvelt, op cit.

100 P Hirst and G Thompson, op cit, p55.

101 C Harman, 'Globalisation', *International Socialism* 2:73 (1996), p7.

102 A Hoogvelt, op cit, p77.

103 *Financial Times*, 1 October 1997.

104 Ibid.

105 World Bank, *Global Economic Prospects and the Developing Countries* (Oxford, 1997).

106 P Hirst and G Thompson, op cit, p68.

107 Ibid.

108 W Ruigrok and R van Tulder, *The Logic of International Restructuring* (London, 1995), p156.

109 R Kiely, 'Globalization, Post-Fordism and the Contemporary Context of Development', *International Sociology* 13:1 (1998), p102.

110 C Harman, op cit, p14.

111 R Kiely, op cit, p105.

112 Ibid.

113 M Korzeniewicz, 'Commodity Chains and Marketing Strategies: Nike and the Global Athletic Footwear Industry,' in G Gereify and M Korzeniewicz (eds), *Commodity Chains and Global Capital* (London, 1994), p259.

114 W Ruigrok and R van Tulder, op cit, p164.

115   A Hoogvelt, op cit, p140.
116   W Ruigrok and R van Tulder, op cit, p151.
117   R Kiely op cit, p104.
118   N Harris, op cit, p192.
119   A Callinicos, op cit, p93.
120   Report from American Express Bank, *The Independent*, 28 February 1998.
121   N Harris, op cit, p30.
122   Datta-Chaudhuri, quoted in T Hewitt, *Industrialization and Development* (Oxford, 1992), p187.
123   R Hinnebusch, *Egyptian Politics Under Sadat* (Cambridge, 1985), pp69-70.
124   R Sandbrook, *The Politics of Africa's Economic Recovery* (Cambridge, 1993), p5.
125   Ibid, ch 3.
126   Ibid, p8.
127   World Bank, *World Development Report 1990* (New York, 1990), p178.
128   *The Guardian*, 6 May 1998.
129   Ibid.
130   *Investment Week*, 21 September 1998.
131   *The Guardian*, 11 May 1998.
132   Ibid.
133   World Bank, *World Development Report 1996* (New York, 1996).
134   ICEM, *Power and Counterpower: The Union Response to Global Capital* (London, 1996), p40.
135   *The Guardian*, 11 May 1998.
136   A Simms of Christian Aid, reported in *The Guardian*, 8 October 1998.
137   Ibid.
138   C Barshefsky, quoted ibid.
139   *Financial Times*, 29 August 1998.
140   *Financial Times*, 23 September 1997.
141   Quoted in J Gray, op cit, p1.
142   *The Economist*, 5 Sepetember 1998.
143   Ibid.
144   *Financial Times*, 23 June 1998.
145   E Zolberg, A Suhrke and S Aguay, *Escape from Violence, the Refugee Crisis in the Developing World* (New York, 1989), p44.
146   *The Guardian*, 7 January 1998.
147   D Hirst and I Beeson, *Sadat* (London, 1981), pp242-243.
148   *Financial Times*, 23 June 1998.
149   Rulers of the dominant world states also face the reality of crisis and of widening inequalities at home. In its 1998 report the UNDP noted for the first time that vast numbers of people in Western countries are in poverty. In developed countries, it noted, more than 37 million people are unemployed, 100 million people are homeless, and 100 million are below the poverty line. Unevenness within such countries is also becoming more pronounced. One US government official has admitted, 'A child born in New York in the 1990s is less likely to live to the age of five than a child in Shanghai. A child born in Bangladesh has better life expectancy than a child born in Harlem.' He warned of the consequences if such problems were not tackled (L Summers, US Deputy Treasury Secretary, quoted in *The Independent*, 10 February 1998).
150   K Moody, *Workers in a Lean World* (London, 1997), p186.
151   Ibid, p209.
152   J Gray, op cit, p207.
153   L Trotsky, op cit, pp107-108.
154   Ibid, p108.

In a class of its own

A review of R McKibbin, **Classes and Cultures: England 1918-1951**
(Oxford, 1998), £25

LINDSEY GERMAN

The cover of Ross McKibbin's book has a photograph of two obviously rich people (he in top hat and tails, she in furs) contentedly walking along a street while ignoring the plight of a homeless man lying on a bench. Like Thomas Dugdale's famous painting of a glittering couple in evening dress who gaze from their Mayfair window as the Jarrow unemployed march passes by, the image encapsulates the popular view of the inter-war period, where the rich got richer and the poor suffered. The information provided by McKibbin produces all the evidence that could be needed to demonstrate the truth of this view, and shows that only by plunging into its second world war in a generation could the world begin to reverse these priorities, end unemployment and start to create a more equal society.

This work is part social history—looking at how different classes behaved in relation to sex, sport, cinema and reading—and part an analysis of class, from the very top with the monarchy down to the working class. All this is interesting enough, but the period covered gives the book a further dimension: its social history has to be set against a British ruling class whose fortunes were declining both sharply and rapidly, and a working class which underwent a process of change in these years which was very dramatic and far reaching. In 1918 Britain emerged victorious from a war which saw its major European rival defeated and faced with revolution. With the exception of Ireland, Britain's colonial empire was still intact. Its transatlantic rival was becoming all powerful but this was still not apparent to many people. By 1951 there was no such ambiguity. The US dominated the Western world economically, politically and increasingly culturally. Britain had been forced to borrow from the US to finance its war effort, and its post-war austerity was in part due to the US calling in the debt. Meanwhile the empire's greatest prize, India, had won independence, and Britain's other colonies were heading the same way.

The traditional working class of the 'workshop of the world' had been in decline throughout the period: mining, shipbuilding and textiles were for much of the inter-war years 'depressed' and economic growth occurred increasingly in new areas—the south and Midlands of England—and in new industries such as motors, aircraft, electrical goods and food processing. For all workers these three decades signalled great change: for example many had access to domestic electricity for the first time, opening up communications such as radio; cinema became the most popular pastime; and the changing world of work meant that women increasingly sought employment in new industries and in clerical jobs which had hardly existed before the First World War.

Britain was (and still is) often described as a very class ridden society. This is not meant in the Marxist sense, that there is an exploited and an exploiter class which defines the whole of society, since this would be equally true of, say, Germany or the US, whatever the superficial differences of politics or culture. Rather it is meant in the sense that the class divisions in Britain seem particularly acute and obvious. They are underlined by, on the one hand, a hereditary peerage and monarchy and by an education system which entrenches archaic privilege both in public schools and in the Oxbridge system; on the other hand, the working class is the oldest and in some ways most ingrained and traditional in the world, and has famously built up layers of defensive networks in order to protect its interests. It is beyond McKibbin's remit to analyse why the class structure in England turned out this way, but he develops a number of important and interesting insights. His view of the monarchy, for example, shows how a combination of luck and opportunism (plus, no doubt, access to great quantities of wealth) allowed the Windsors to maintain their hold through this period. The dullness of George V, his preoccupation with the minutiae of etiquette and country house living and his lack of interest in any wider intellectual or cultural questions, did not prevent him from very astutely preventing his cousin the Russian Tsar Nicholas, who had been deposed by the Russian Revolution, from coming to live in England. The king's private secretary wrote to the foreign secretary in April 1917 that 'the residence of the ex-Emperor and Empress would be strongly resented by the public, and would undoubtedly compromise the position of the King and Queen'.[1] The monarchy was careful never to openly alienate workers or the labour movement, according to the author, even though the royal family's instincts were Tory to the last and even though they were part of a wider ruling class which, in the 1920s particularly, was engaged in open class war.

What of the working class? It was the first developed working class in the world. The size of the working class and its relative social weight were unique in a country where the peasantry had been destroyed by industrial development and modern agriculture. The working class had also developed a fairly distinctive lifestyle and cultural life; industrial villages such as those around coal mining or the industrial areas of the big cities typified this lifestyle with their terraced housing, pubs and working men's clubs, keenness on sports and (except in the textile areas) a rigid sexual division of labour. This 'traditional' working class life changed in the period described by McKibbin. Of course, it was never as 'traditional' as all that: roughly it dated from the last quarter of the 19th century to the first quarter of the 20th. But the pressures of war, slump and capitalist competition were to destroy it forever and to change the ideas and attitudes of the working class. Even in the inter-war period those ideas and attitudes were very contradictory. English workers are often thought of as insular and xenophobic, but in many respects their industrial background, with its lack of religious or conservative family ties (compared to most of continental Europe, for example), made them outward looking, adventurous and open to new cultural influences. The English were, for example, the greatest cinema goers per head in the world in the 1930s and 1940s, and this attendance was heavily concentrated in the working class and lower middle classes:

*In 1950 the average Englishman and woman went to the pictures 28 times per year, more than 10 percent of **total** world cinema attendance, a per capita figure not even exceeded in the United States. Throughout the 1930s there were 18-19 million weekly attendances... By 1945 it was 30 million. In 1946, the year when cinema attendance was at its highest, one-third of the whole population went to the pictures at least once a week, and there were a total of 1,635 million attendances.*[2]

The dominant influence in cinema along with music and dancing was heavily Americanised and this was generally welcomed by working people. They took to various forms of American popular music from 1918 onwards, including jazz influenced black music; the dances which became staples of English ballroom dancing (itself a worldwide cultural phenomenon) such as the quickstep and foxtrot were derived from American 'rag' dances. The huge dance halls such as the Hammersmith Palais and the Streatham Locarno came into their own in the 1920s and

1930s. The English often preferred American films to the indigenous variety, especially in the 1930s, because they were thought 'vigorous, materialist and democratic. Those who disliked British films disliked them because they were none of these. Most widely disliked was the accent of the actors and, even more, the actresses'. McKibbin continues: 'The working class part of the audience was also unsympathetic to the extreme emotional restraint of many British films—even the most widely admired, like *Brief Encounter* (1945), which was by almost universal consent a "classic" British movie, yet not really popular in England outside the suburbs. People were offended by Celia Johnson's "prissiness" and found her moral dilemma incomprehensible'.[3]

That English workers could accept much of American culture without accepting some of the worst aspects of US society was demonstrated during the Second World War when, despite the British authorities trying to maintain US army segregation between black and white soldiers, this was repeatedly opposed by ordinary people:

> There were several well-publicised cases, some violent, where English civilians took the side of black GIs against white American servicemen. Both the British government and the American authorities were compelled to recognise indigenous attitudes: on arrival white Americans were warned that segregation did not operate in Britain and urged to accept that. The issue of segregation was not marginal to Anglo-American relations: it was widely discussed, widely disliked and, outside official circles, did not enhance the appearance of America in English eyes.[4]

English people—again in contrast to many other nationalities—had relatively weak adherence to religion. This adherence went into steady decline during the inter-war years, and much of the supposed commitment, especially to the Anglican church, was only nominal. Women adhered instead to various forms of spiritualism, astrology or other forms of mysticism:

> The social anthropologist Geoffrey Gorer thought a substantial proportion of the population 'holds a view of the universe which can most properly be designated as magical'—a passive cosmology where there was no perceived connection between effort and outcome. That so many more women than men— especially married working class women—held to such a cosmology suggests among many of them a real social powerlessness, a feeling that they had little control over their lives.[5]

Working class women certainly lacked control over their sexuality. Indeed contradictory and often hypocritical attitudes to sexuality in

England seem to characterise this period. English people seemed very keen on chastity outside marriage (in the early 1950s, 52 percent were opposed to men and 63 percent opposed to women having any premarital sex) but themselves did not follow such strictures, so in 1938-1939 some 30 percent of all women conceived their first child before marriage. At the same time many women clearly felt that sex was something they had to endure reluctantly rather than to enjoy—'working class women repeatedly expressed either hostility or indifference to marital sexuality'.[6] Although this changed between 1918 and 1951, and probably changed even more dramatically in the two decades afterwards, it was clearly a widespread view. The other side of the coin, however, was a more open attitude to non-sexual relationships between men and women. McKibbin describes how what was often called the 'puritanical' attitude to sex had this positive effect: 'in the early 1950s more than half the English thought it possible for people of the opposite sex to have non-sexual friendships a proportion unlikely to be found in many other European countries.' But he goes on, 'The negative consequence of puritanism was a sexual prurience and a delight in pornography famous throughout Europe'.[7]

The contrast between the attitudes of the various classes is shown most dramatically in relation to sport. This section is one of the strongest in the book, perhaps reflecting the overwhelming importance of sport in this period. McKibbin writes:

> The English were a sports loving people, and that was one of their characteristics which outsiders immediately identified. But they loved different sports; only cricket is a possible exception. At the extremes some sports were so socially specific as to be undefinable except by those who played them. And at all levels the sport people played or followed was, like what they read, determined by class, modified, though not by much, by place of birth or residence.[8]

Yet the history of sport in these years can also be seen as a microcosm of British capitalism. A country which led the world in inventing and developing sports in the 19th and early 20th centuries suddenly found other nations catching up and overtaking it. The extremely popular football clubs made money for directors but nothing was invested in new or improved grounds. England began to win much less:

> Throughout this period one of the striking features of English sport was the decline in its international competitiveness. Since every major international sport, with the exception of basketball, was English (or, in the case of golf, British) in origin; since, therefore, England had enormous advantages in experience and tradition, such decline was for the English surprising and depressing.[9]

Much of this decline can be attributed to the systems of amateur and professional players in games such as cricket and golf, which were both incredibly snobbish in their disdain for any sort of 'professionalism'—working people trying to make a living from their sporting skill—and terribly wasteful of talent as a result. It is also clear, however, that this system, coupled with a reluctance of the state to spend large amounts of money training and promoting sportsmen and women, meant that England was increasingly at a disadvantage competitively against countries such as the US and pre-war Germany which provided far more resources. The British relied on the traditional structures of sport, the public schools and universities, and sport sponsored by private industry.

The same piecemeal approach could be seen with education, where McKibbin describes how the grammar school system between the wars was quite inefficient in terms of the needs of British capitalism. The schools were beyond the reach of most working class children, but even those who attended them found them quite unsuitable training for later life—they left both underqualified and overqualified, as the author puts it. They were underqualified because the schools refused to teach any practical skills, such as shorthand typing, which might be useful in gaining work. They were overqualified because they were trained for the matriculation system, needed for university entrance—but before 1945 hardly any grammar school children went to university.

The structures of life in Britain were, in virtually every respect, different for members of different classes and very heavily influenced by class considerations. If these seemed particularly archaic this was perhaps to do with Britain's original pre-eminence as a capitalist power; by the 1920s and 30s the ruling class felt its decline but was hampered by many of its institutions from changing rapidly. The Second World War altered some of that, but the previous decades also saw substantial change. The growth of a salaried middle class and of a clerical workforce, the advent of mass media, communications such as cars, aircraft and telephones can all date their mass use from towards the end of the period studied here. The effect of mass unemployment and migration to find work—'not dead but gone to Slough', as the Welsh used to say—also broke up the old traditional working class communities around mining and shipbuilding.

It is here that McKibbin's analysis is flawed in a way which, by and large, does not detract from his study but which makes for an unsatisfactory conclusion. His assumption is certainly that the working class can and does change during the period he studies, but he always assumes that this working class is composed of manual workers. He states quite explicitly that clerical workers, even the low paid shop workers or clerks, were middle class: 'What mattered was occupation and the social aspirations and manners which occupation demanded. On this ground, and one other— their very strong sense of not being working class—those in clerical work must be regarded as middle class'.[10] Now it is true that probably the majority of clerical workers thought of themselves as in some way 'a cut above' manual workers in the inter-war years. It is also true that they very often worked in proximity to but segregated from manual workers, in offices attached to factories, much more than their equivalents would now. But that was already beginning to change in McKibbin's period. There were typing pools and large accounts offices, telephone exchanges, American style shops such as Woolworth's. The employees in such work were in most respects becoming more like manual workers in terms of wages, conditions and control over their work (McKibbin himself mentions the bedaux system or 'time and motion' studies). With the benefit of hindsight we can see this process of 'proletarianisation' has become much greater advanced to include bank clerks, many finance and insurance workers, health and education workers as part of a class which is exploited and which has no fundamental difference in interests, income or lifestyles from its manual counterparts.

A failure to understand white collar workers as part of the working class might not appear to matter but its weakness is revealed in McKibbin's conclusions. He sees the working class as a declining class (which it is if we simply judge it by manual workers) and therefore sees 1951 as its high point. Manual workers had come out of the war in employment, better off and having elected a government which supposedly represented them. The middle class, having done very well during the early 1930s, was now relatively worse off, according to this view. McKibbin talks of the traditional working class having been recreated in the 1940s and this leading to the Labour landslide. Its decline led to the decline of Labourism.

Since then, however, we have seen the biggest rise in trade unionism ever (reaching its high point in 1979), a wave of strikes in the early 1970s involving both 'traditional' and 'new' working class militants, and more recently the beginning of reorganisation following the major defeats of the 1980s. In 1997 Labour won its biggest landslide ever, largely from working class votes. The history of that modern working class and, hopefully, its future struggles is still to be written.

However, that is outside the range of this book. Its conceptual weakness in its definition of class does not prevent it covering a whole range of issues about how people lived and worked in these years, how women coped with pregnancy or debt, how workers distrusted the union leaders, how working class children's talent in writing or expressing themselves was ignored or marginalised. It also demonstrates the elitist, patronising and authoritarian way in which the ruling class tried to maintain its rule and how ordinary people found many ways to avoid or circumvent such restrictions. Some things don't change. This book is a valuable history of the specific period; it is also there at the birth of a working class we can recognise today.

Notes

1   Ross McKibbin, *Classes and Cultures: England 1918-1951* (Oxford, 1998), p7.
2   Ibid, p419.
3   Ibid, pp433-434.
4   Ibid, p525.
5   Ibid, pp291-292.
6   Ibid, pp296-297.
7   Ibid, p327.
8   Ibid, p528.
9   Ibid, p377.
10   Ibid, p45.

John Reed: reporting on the revolution

A review of J Newsinger (ed), **Shaking the World: John Reed's Revolutionary Journalism** *(Bookmarks, 1998), £11.95*

JUDY COX

At its best, journalism can help to undermine the ideology of the ruling class, revealing the connections between different aspects of the system, the role played by apparently neutral institutions of the state and the potential of workers' struggles to achieve change. John Reed, a US journalist born in 1887, was perhaps one of the greatest exponents of such journalism. His account of the Russian Revolution, *Ten Days that Shook the World*, is one the best descriptions of that revolution ever written, and Lenin himself recommended it unreservedly. However, John Reed recorded and participated in great struggles beyond Russia, across the American coalfields and the *haciendas* of Mexico. His writings are, therefore, a testimony to the power of committed journalism as well as to the struggles which he witnessed.

John Reed was born into a well to do family but the years in which he grew up, the first decades of the 20th century, were years of growing criticism of, and resistance to, the development of US capitalism. The 'robber barons' were forging business empires at home and the US state was forging its empire abroad in wars against Spain, Cuba and the Philippines. The growing revulsion at this increasingly naked and brutal drive for profits found popular expression in literature, for example in the novels of Upton Sinclair and Jack London which sold millions of copies. Even the acclaimed novelist Henry James wrote that the US was 'rank with each variety of the poison-plant of the money passion'.[1] Alongside the politically committed novelists were a new breed of journalists—the muckrakers—who contributed to the atmosphere of protest.

The year John Reed graduated from Harvard, 1910, was also a year in which the US stood on the brink of a period of tempestuous class struggle. In this infectious political atmosphere it was not surprising that a well educated young man from a comfortable background should start working for a radical magazine, *The Masses*.

It was as a reporter for *The Masses* that John Reed first encountered the class struggle in the flesh when he was sent to cover a strike by silk weavers in Paterson, New Jersey, in 1913. The forces involved in the strike were typical of many strikes in the US during this decade. On one side were the employers, backed up by the violence of the police, the courts and private 'detectives'. On the other were a desperate group of workers, many of them immigrants, whose only support was the Industrial Workers of the World. The IWW was a revolutionary syndicalist organisation which helped the Paterson strikers build rank and file solidarity so successfully that by March 1913 some 25,000 workers were striking. John Reed arrived in April and was almost immediately arrested, eventually finding himself in prison with the IWW leader, Big Bill Haywood. Reed described with great power and passion the treatment that the striking men, women and children received, how they were beaten off the pickets lines, arrested in their thousands and imprisoned in inhuman conditions. The scale of the arrests in Paterson was one of the highest in US labour history. In one trial a women in the audience was sentenced to 60 days in prison for smiling, and another for 30 days for gasping at this sentence! By the end of the strike five strikers had also been murdered. Reed's articles proved to be so popular that one Paterson policeman later complained that 'jailing one lousy poet' gave the IWW more publicity than jailing hundreds of strikers.

The weavers were eventually beaten back to work but the Paterson strike turned out to be a mere preliminary to the struggles which then erupted. In September 1913 the United Mine Workers of America took on J D Rockefeller's Colorado Fuel and Iron Company. The conditions in the mines were appalling, union members were summarily sacked and union organisers were regularly assassinated. The miners were fighting for an eight hour day, a 10 percent pay increase, union recognition, the limitation of company fraud and the enforcement of Colorado's mining laws! Despite a blizzard, all strikers and their families were immediately evicted from their company owned homes. The union established tent colonies to house 11,000 workers but these were frequently fired on by company guards. The strike reached a crisis point in April 1914 when National Guardsmen attacked the Ludlow colony with machine guns. Women and children hid in cellars dug under the tents and, when the guards set fire to their tents, some were burnt alive. At least two women and 11 children were killed. A union organiser, Louis Tikas, was captured and shot out of hand.

Reed arrived in Colorado shortly after the massacre. He described the

tragic scene at the camp where baby carriages and children's toys lay
riddled with bullets. Reed also wrote about how the miners responded—
by launching a virtual insurrection in the coalfields. The miners' union
openly armed the strikers and in a series of ferocious attacks scabs and
guards were killed and mines dynamited. Reed described how news of
the massacre spread like wildfire:

> *In three hours every striker for 50 miles in either direction knows that the*
> *militia and mine guards had burned women and children to death. Monday*
> *night they started, with all the guns they could lay their hands on, for the*
> *scene of the action at Ludlow. All night long the roads were filled with ragged*
> *mobs of armed men pouring towards the Black Hills. And not only strikers*
> *went. In Aguilar, Walsenburg and Trinidad, clerks, cab drivers, chauffeurs,*
> *school teachers, and even bankers seized their guns and started for the front.*
> *It was as if the fire started at Ludlow had set the whole country aflame.*[2]

At this point the federal government intervened, not to protect the
strikers but to protect the mine owners from them. Despite widespread
outrage at the massacre and big demonstrations in solidarity with the
strikers, the strike was defeated. For Reed, it was a 'transforming experience', similar to that which George Orwell underwent in Barcelona in
1937.[3] When Reed reported from the strike, he called his article *The
Colorado War* to drive home to his audience the violence that was being
mobilised against the strikers. The article caused such outrage among
those who supported the mine owners that some bookstores refused to
sell the magazine which carried it. In the article, Reed explained the
appalling provocation which drove ordinary workers to take up arms. He
pointed out that the workers were not revolutionaries, but were simply
fighting for a living wage and safety at work and for the implementation
of the law. Reed explained how at every turn the workers were pushed
towards militancy by the intransigence of the mine owners and the brutality of the tactics they used.

Reed also described how for generations miners fought back and were
defeated, each defeat leading to their replacement with more recent
immigrant workers. He gave a brilliant sense of how those divisions
were eroded by the experience of living in the Ludlow camp: 'There
were more than 1,200 people there, divided in 21 nationalities, under-
going the marvellous experience of learning that all men are alike. When
they had been living together for two weeks, the petty race prejudices
and misunderstandings that had been fostered between them by the coal
companies for so many years began to break down'.[4] *The Colorado War*
exposes the reality behind the American dream—a reality of savage
repression by the ruling class and working class unity forged in the heat

of the struggle. It conveys an unforgettable sense of how militant the US working class tradition really is.

Before his trip to Colorado, Reed reported from Mexico which was in the turmoil of a revolution which, as John Newsinger points out in his introduction, was 'one of the great social revolutions of the 20th century'. When Reed arrived there in December 1913, General Huerta, who was installed by a military coup, was facing a rebellion by the Constitutionalists, an uneasy alliance between middle class liberals and the working class and peasant armies led by Pancho Villa and Emiliano Zapata. Reed was unequivocally on the side of the Villistas and Zapatistas, to the point of having to run for his life during a battle at La Cadena. Reed's articles from Mexico revealed the real roots of the revolution in the poverty of the land starved peons, who worked like draft horses on the big *haciendas,* and their growing desire for a representative government. He also launched a powerful polemic against the growing movement for US intervention in Mexico. He argued fiercely against the idea that the Mexican Revolution was merely a 'comic opera', asserting instead that it was the slowly accumulated grievances of the peons that had burst into life and that US intervention would inevitably mean crushing the newly awakened democratic aspirations of the Mexican people.

In September 1914 Reed wrote an article on the outbreak of the First World War, which he called *The Traders' War.* His article was a resounding condemnation of that war:

> *We who are socialists, must hope—we may even expect—that out of this horror of bloodshed and dire destruction will come far reaching social changes—and a long step forward towards our goal of peace among men.*
>
> *But we must not be duped by this editorial buncombe about liberalism going forth to holy war against tyranny.*
>
> *This is not our war.*[5]

'This is not our war'—this was the theme he returned to again and again. He described how right across Europe young men were intimidated, bullied and shamed into 'volunteering' to fight, how Harrods department store loaded a truck with young clerks and sent them to the recruiting office with a big sign on the side: 'Harrods' Gift to the Empire'.[6] In other articles Reed attacked the war fever growing in the US: 'I know what war means. I have been with the armies of all the belligerents except one, and I have seen men die, and go mad, and lie in hospitals suffering hell; but there is a worse thing than that. War means an ugly mob madness, crucifying the truth tellers, choking the artists, sidetracking reforms, revolutions and the working of social forces'.[7]

The highlights of this collection of essays are, perhaps inevitably, Reed's reports from the Russian Revolution. His writings on Russia in this volume are not merely exciting accounts of the greatest revolution in world history, although that alone would be well worth reading. Reed combined his narrative accounts with insights which can help us refute some of the key criticisms levelled at the revolution. For example, Reed wrote that it was fashionable to consider the revolution as a mere adventure. He replied, 'Adventure it is, and one of the most splendid mankind ever embarked on, sweeping into history at the head of the toiling masses and staking everything on their vast and simple ideas'.[8] Reed explained how the success of the revolution lay in the fact 'that the Kerensky government absolutely ignored the desires of the masses as expressed in the Bolshevik programme of peace, land and workers' control of industry', rather than in any skilful scheming by the Bolsheviks. He explained how disgust with the impotence of Kerensky's Provisional Government led to the 'astounding growth of the Bolsheviki' and how the Bolshevik Party was the 'ultimate political expression of the popular will'. In addition Reed emphasised the involvement of the masses in the revolutionary process: 'The entire insurrection is a stirring spectacle of proletarian mass organisation, action, bravery and generosity.' The revolution which Reed witnessed aroused the enthusiasm and participation of the masses and was not a coup undertaken by a small group of fanatics behind the backs of the working classes. Reed pointed out that, contrary to the image created in the bourgeois press, the Bolsheviks were reluctant to use violence against their opponents, how many of the reactionary Junkers were captured and released on their word of honour only to take up arms again, and how papers opposed to the Bolsheviks were allowed to publish. In addition, Reed was very clear that, 'if the Bolsheviki do not rise, *the propertied class will make a coup d'état at the Constituent Assembly!*'[9] In other words, the choice facing Russia in 1917 was not that between violent revolution and peaceful parliamentarianism, but that between the Bolsheviks or the White armies, socialism or barbarism.

Reed described momentous events: the opening of the All-Russian Congress of Soviets, the storming of the Winter Palace and the frontline fighting between the Red Guard and the White armies. Any socialist reading these articles will experience a thrill when reading these lines, written for *The Liberator* in November 1918:

The masses are in power... And on the morning of 13 November, after the defeat of Kerensky's Cossack army, Lenin and Trotsky sent through me to the revolutionary proletariat of the world this message:
    Comrades! Greetings from the first proletariat republic of the world. We call you to arms for the international social revolution.[10]

Reed's 'A Picture of Petrograd' is a brilliant vision of a great city in the throes of social revolution. In another article championing the cause of the revolution printed in *The Liberator* during the German Revolution in 1918-1919, Reed points out that, while the Allies' military power merely broke the German offensive in the west, Soviet Russia conquered Imperial Germany completely and so ended the war with the German Revolution, because the rising proletariat was so much more powerful an enemy than the greatest military machine.

According to one witness, Reed arrived in Petrograd a rebel and left a revolutionary. As a revolutionary Reed was convinced that it was his duty to take the fight home to US workers and campaign against foreign intervention in Russia. But back in the US Reed found himself in the middle of a witch hunt against socialists. This was the era of what Gabriel Kolko has called 'political capitalism',[11] where the huge industrial empires increasingly mobilised the power of the state to stem revolt from below. Reed described with understandable outrage the suppression of the socialist press, the horrific race riots of 1919 and the wholesale deportations of striking workers, a process which culminated in the Palmer Raids of January 1919. Confronted by this onslaught Reed embarked on a series of articles, published in a revolutionary paper, the *New York Communist*, which exposed the reality of 'capitalist democracy in America'. In these articles Reed explained the Marxist analysis of the state and refuted the idea that the US state was different because of its constitutional guarantee of the right to life, liberty and the pursuit of happiness. He revealed how the concentration of wealth in the hands of the capitalists led to the development of 'dollar diplomacy' and the increasing power of big business over the institutions of the state. He described the socialist ideas which arrived with successive generations of immigrants and how they fell prey to reformism: 'Even after the capitalist class in America had learned that government is not carried on in legislatures, but in banks and chambers of commerce, the workers still believed that political democracy could salve the problems of the wage earners'.[12]

Throughout his writings, Reed expressed his contempt for the American Federation of Labour and its exclusion of unskilled workers. But in an article he wrote for the Communist International he also pointed out the fatal flaw in the revolutionary syndicalism of the IWW. The IWW led inspiring struggles under its banner of 'One Big Union'. Wherever workers fought, the Wobblies (as IWW members were known) were there to support them, black and white, men and women. Yet for all its heroism, 'from all the assaults upon the factory industries, from all the great strikes in the East, there is barely a skeleton of organisation left to tell the tale'.[13] He concluded that the IWW was a powerful propaganda centre, but not a force which could win over the majority of workers. He also revealed how the Wobblies' rejection of 'politics', their exclusive focus on industrial militancy, left them vulnerable when faced with the onslaught of the capitalist state. So, for example, 'on the charge of "obstructing the war", the IWW was decapitated'.[14]

In the spring of 1919 Reed began editing the *New York Communist* and led one of the two rival US Communist Parties which were established that year. While the two parties squabbled about who were the real Bolsheviks, the AFL, in spite of its craftism, was leading mass struggles. At the height of the 1919 steel strike, for example, 365,000 workers were out, but the Communists failed to build any influence over the workers involved. State repression continued unabated—in one case three men convicted of distributing leaflets against intervention in Russia were sentenced to 20 years in prison—and it almost destroyed the Communist Parties. Reed himself escaped arrest only by returning to Russia, where he contracted typhus and, due to a lack of medicine, died on 17 October 1920, a victim of the Western blockade of revolutionary Russia.

As the articles in this volume demonstrate, Reed remained committed to the prospect of revolution to the end of his all too short life. This collection gives a flavour of the class struggle which followed the First World War in Russia, then capitalism's weakness link, and also in the US, then emerging as the greatest world power. John Reed also analysed the political issues which lay at the heart of the victory of that struggle in Russia and its bitter defeat in the US. His burning criticisms of US imperialism, his consistent condemnation of the terrible racism of US society and his faith in the power of working class struggle are threads which run unbroken through this volume of revolutionary journalism at its best.

Notes

1   Quoted in H Zinn, *A People's History of the United States* (Harper & Row, 1980), p315.
2   J Newsinger (ed), *Shaking the World: John Reed's Revolutionary Journalism* (Bookmarks, 1998), p45.
3   Ibid, pxviii.
4   Ibid, p22.
5   Ibid, p79.
6   Ibid, p83.
7   Ibid, p93.
8   Ibid, p120.
9   Ibid, p121.
10   Ibid, p128.
11   H Zinn, op cit, p342.
12   J Reed, op cit, p190.
13   Ibid, p229.
14   Ibid, p236.

The resistible rise of Adolf Hitler

A review of I Kershaw, **Hitler 1889-1936: Hubris** *(Allen Lane, 1998), £20*

KEVIN OVENDEN

How did a talentless, unemployed house painter come to lead Europe's most powerful country, smash the best organised working class in the world and establish a monstrous dictatorship?

The first volume of Ian Kershaw's biography of Hitler, *Hitler: 1889-1936*, adds to our understanding of how the Nazis grew from being a fringe sect to an organisation which could seize power in January 1933. The book is a major undertaking, running to over 700 pages in length. Kershaw is one of the foremost historians of the Third Reich and is the author of numerous books and articles including a pathbreaking study of attitudes to the Nazis in Bavaria, *Popular Opinion and Political Dissent in the Third Reich*, and a useful survey of key debates among historians about the nature of Hitler's regime, *The Nazi Dictatorship: Problems and Perspectives of Interpretation*.

Kershaw has recently gained a wider audience as the historical adviser to the BBC's *Nazis—A Warning From History* series. He has done a great service in bringing a wealth of historical research together in this volume and compressing it into a highly readable account of Hitler's rise to power.

The book is written as a biography. As such the interaction between the personality of Hitler and the historical forces which shaped him and which he influenced is at the heart of it. Kershaw describes Hitler's upbringing as the son of an Austrian customs official, his schooling and family background. But he rejects the fashion for reducing historical events and biographical writing to the supposed psychological traits of individuals.

'The conditions for the "making of Adolf Hitler",' as Kershaw puts it, were his experiences of the November Revolution of 1918 which sparked mutiny and ended Germany's participation in the First World War, overthrew the Kaiser and led to the creation of workers' and soldiers' councils across Germany. Hitler was in Munich, which was to become one of the key centres of the revolution in 1919. He was a committed German nationalist and was horrified by the display of workers' power. His embittered reaction summed up in an extreme form the trauma of the middle classes who feared that the Russian Revolution of October 1917 might be repeated in Germany. The German Revolution and the counter-revolution, which finally triumphed in 1923, left a searing mark on Hitler. In later speeches he would constantly denounce the 'November criminals', the social democratic leaders he held responsible for the revolutionary upsurge and fall of the Kaiser. Even after he had seized power and dismantled every working class organisation, his fear of another 'stab in the back', a workers' uprising, influenced his policies.

He became involved in the nationalist, anti-Semitic groups which agitated against the revolution. The counter-revolution directed by the German state was the making of him. As Kershaw puts it:

Without the changed conditions, the product of a lost war, a revolution and a pervasive sense of national humiliation, Hitler would have remained a nobody. His main ability by far, as he came to realise during the course of 1919, was that in the prevailing circumstances he could inspire an audience which shared his basic political feelings, by the way he spoke, by the force of his rhetoric, by the very power of his prejudice, by the conviction he conveyed that there was a way out of Germany's plight, and that only the way he outlined was the road to national rebirth.[1]

The German Revolution left Hitler with a visceral, almost pathological hatred of Marxism, which he equated with the Social Democratic and Communist parties. It is one of the strengths of Kershaw's book that he shows the centrality of 'anti-Marxism' to Hitler's world view and integrates it into his account of the Nazis' growth in the early 1930s. In so doing, he covers a number of key historical issues which have been the subject of recent controversy. It is, therefore, inevitable that Kershaw presents arguments and emphases with which one can disagree. But this book is significant because it broadly confirms the classical Marxist analysis of the rise of the Nazis, even though Kershaw is no Marxist and his sympathies are with the social democrats' doomed attempts to stabilise 'normal capitalism' during the Great Depression rather than with revolutionary attempts to overthrow it.

I want to focus on a small number of interrelated issues where Kershaw's interpretation supports the Marxist case, but which also show the limitations of not having a Marxist theory. These centre on the class character of the Nazi movement.

Kershaw provides powerful evidence which refutes the argument put by US historian Daniel Goldhagen, among others, that the Nazis came to power because their lurid anti-Semitism attracted mass support from the German people, who were in some way predisposed to the 'elimination' of the Jews. Kershaw compares Hitler's speeches in 1930, the year of the Nazis' first electoral breakthrough, with those that went before:

In the early 1920s, Hitler's speeches had been dominated by vicious attacks on the Jews. In the later 1920s, the question of 'living-space' became the central theme. In the election campaign of 1930, Hitler seldom spoke explicitly of Jews. The crude tirades of the early 1920s were missing altogether. 'Living-space' figured more prominently, posed against the alternative international competition for markets. But it was not omnipresent as it had been in 1927-1928. The key theme now was the collapse of Germany under parliamentary democracy and party government into a divided people with separate and conflicting interests, which only the NSDAP [Nazi Party] could overcome by creating a new unity of the nation, transcending class, estate and profession.[2]

Hitler was prepared to relegate anti-Semitism from centre stage in his speeches in his efforts to build out of the despair wrought by the economic collapse of the 1930s. But anti-Semitism was at the centre of his and the Nazis' ideology. This was not simply a product of Hitler's and other leading Nazis' graduation through the anti-Semitic right in the early 1920s. It rested on the class character of the Nazi movement.

Hitler appealed above all to the middle classes who were ruined by the crisis, squeezed between big business on the one hand and organised labour on the other. So as well as lashing out at Marxism, he also tried to reflect the petty bourgeoisie's confused opposition to big capital. It was a contradiction made all the more intense by the Nazis' attempts to gain the backing of big business and the political establishment. Hitler had tried and failed to launch a right wing coup in 1923 and the experience had convinced him he would need to find a 'legal route' to power with the support of at least some sections of the ruling class and state rather than their oppositon . Anti-Semitism provided the 'ideological cement' holding together the anti-working class and pseudo anti-capitalist messages, and binding the chaotic Nazi Party itself. Kershaw writes:

Nazi diabolisation of the Jews enabled them to be portrayed as both the representatives of rapacious big capital and of pernicious and brutal Bolshevism. Most Germans did not go along with such crude images. Nor were they likely to become involved in, or approve of, physical violence directed at individual Jews and their property. But dislike of Jews extended far beyond Nazi sympathisers...

It was no coincidence, for instance, that one of the most viciously anti-Semitic Nazi sub-organisations was the Fighting League of the Commercial Middle Class, where small traders campaigned against department stores that they claimed to be largely in Jewish hands.[3]

Anti-Semitic bile, in the minds of Hitler and the core of the Nazi Party, was not simply a convenient ploy to be modulated according to the mood of the electorate. It was, from the beginning, the most potent feature of their vision of a 'national racial community' which would transcend class divisions not through abolishing classes but by getting rid of any group that was not part of the nation. Hitler berated Otto Strasser, a Nazi he felt was taking the party's selective anti-capitalist rhetoric too seriously, just before the September 1930 elections which saw the Nazi vote rise from 2.6 percent to 18.3 percent:

'There is only one possible kind of revolution, and it is not economic or political or social, but racial,' he avowed. Pushed on his attitude to big business, Hitler made plain that there could be no question for him of socialisation or worker [sic] control. The only priority was for a strong state to ensure that production was carried out in the national interest.[4]

The contradiction between the promise of a social revolution which would put the 'little man' at the centre of a harmonious national community and the determination of Hitler to preserve capitalist social relations meant there was always pent up frustration within the Nazis' ranks and among their supporters. This frustration provided the reservoir for ever more radicalised bouts of anti-Semitic violence throughout the 1930s.

It also brought chaos and the constant threat of splits within the Nazi Party. The tensions increased as the Nazis grew to over 1.4 million members in 1932 with 400,000 in the paramilitary SA. The deepening crisis drove millions of people enraged at 'the system' towards the Nazis, but the closer Hitler got to power, the more he sought the backing of the political and business establishments which were the main object of people's fury. Kershaw discusses the debates within the German capitalist class throughout the latter half of 1932 and beginning of 1933 about how to deal with Hitler. The title of the chapter itself, 'Levered Into Power', makes clear the role of those at the top of society in hoisting Hitler into power even though two thirds of Germans voted against him. He gives a careful account of how the political elite, with President Hindenburg at the centre, decided to offer Hitler the chancellorship, but with only a minority of Nazis in a coalition cabinet. He provides less insight into the shifting attitudes of the wider ruling class. This is in part because he relies on the work of Henry Ashby Turner, whose *German Big Business and the Rise of Hitler* tries to downplay the support Hitler got from significant sections of industry. So Kershaw writes, 'As January [1933] progressed, it would prove to be the big landowners, through their lobbying organisation, the Reichslandbund (Reich Agrarian League), rather than the "captains of industry", who emerged as the mortal enemies of the Schleicher cabinet [the last government before Hitler's] and the leading proponents of the elevation of Hitler to the chancellorship'.[5]

But he explicitly rejects the notion that pre-capitalist forces brought Hitler to power. He shows that the big landowners were thoroughly capitalist, and writes:

These were no pre-industrial leftovers, but—however reactionary their political aims—modern lobbies working to further their vested interests in an authoritarian system. In the final drama, the agrarians and the army were more influential than big business in engineering Hitler's takeover. But big business...had significantly contributed to the undermining of democracy which was the necessary prelude to Hitler's success.[6]

If Kershaw underplays the extent and depth of support for Hitler among important industrialists like steel magnate Fritz Thyssen and how early this support came, he does bring to the fore the uncertainty within the German ruling class in 1932-1933. They had stumbled through a succession of regimes, led by Heinrich Bruening, Franz von Papen and finally General Kurt von Schleicher. Each had ruled by presidential decree and had attempted to break the organised working class, especially the Communist Party which had attracted mass support among the unemployed: 'But the ruling groups did not have the mass support to maximise their ascendancy and destroy once and for all the power of organised labour.' Divisions within the ruling class were so great that 'big business was at first divided in its opinion of the Schleicher government. Its early fears of the "Red General", regarded by business leaders as a crypto-socialist, had not materialised'.[7]

It was the failure of traditional counter-revolutionary methods— above all, the fear that the army would split if called upon to launch a coup—which pushed even bourgeois leaders like von Papen, who had opposed Hitler being brought into the government in August 1932, to back a Hitler chancellorship. The bulk of the ruling class did not trust Hitler. They feared the Nazis' bastardised socialist rhetoric could spill over into attacks on property. They much preferred orderly repression by the army to the furious outpourings of the Brownshirts. But they had a 'partial identity' of interests with Hitler. Both wanted to 'destroy Marxism', to shatter the working class. Both wanted to overturn the Versailles Treaty and restore German military power, especially in central and eastern Europe. So in the words of Franz von Papen, they 'hired him'.

Kershaw slams the decision of Germany's rulers to hand state power to the Nazis. He shows how they underestimated the strength of Hitler's movement which used its position as a minority within the government rapidly, not only to repress the working class parties and trade unions, with the full support of the capitalist class, but also to outlaw the openly capitalist parties and replace conservative politicians with Nazis by the middle of 1934. He writes of their 'miscalculations' in, among other things, 'failing to impose a hefty jail sentence' on Hitler for his attempted putsch of 1923. He goes on:

> But those miscalculations...were not random acts. They were the miscalculations of a political class determined to inflict what injury it could...on the new, detested or at best merely tolerated democratic republic. The anxiety to destroy democracy rather than the keenness to bring the Nazis to power was what triggered the complex developments that led to Hitler's chancellorship.[8]

This begs the question of why the German ruling class chose this course. Here Kershaw's own standpoint leaves him hedging over the answer. He traces the hostility of the 'German elites' to democracy and the organised working class back to the birth of the Weimar Republic in the revolutionary years of 1918-1923. He talks of the particular 'mentalities' among Germany's middle and ruling classes forged then and previously under the Kaiser. But he quickly adds:

> Even so, Hitler was no inexorable product of a German 'special path', no logical culmination of long-term trends in specifically German culture and ideology. Nor was he a mere 'accident' in the course of German history.[9]

Kershaw can rule out the possiblity that Hitler's seizure of power was an accident or the product of centuries old 'cultural forces', but he does not provide a rounded positive account of the process because he fails to appreciate the nature of the crisis Germany experienced in the early

1930s and the class struggle it unleashed. For Kershaw, the alternatives in 1932-1933 were between democracy and dictatorship. But the crisis meant the rule of capital had become inconsistent with continuing bourgeois democracy. The choice was between the continuation of capitalism, through the most barbarous means, and workers imposing their own solution on society. There is little discussion of the workers' movement in the early 1930s in Kershaw's book. Where there is, it is usually to describe the demoralising and atomising impact of mass unemployment. Yet the Nazis were not the only beneficiaries of the crisis. The left, particularly the Communist Party, grew. Leon Trotsky's magnificent writings on Germany spell out not only how the Communist Party could have broken the back of the Nazi movement through a policy of united action with the Social Democrats, despite their leaders' opposition to it. Trotsky also shows how, as happened in France three years later, checking the Nazis could allow the working class to move from the defensive to the offensive.

This failure to consider the full impact of the crisis on all classes and political forces in Germany is part of a wider weakness. Kershaw describes how the Nazis won support, and the reaction of Germany's 'elites', but he does not attempt to give a theory of fascism as a political movement. Frustratingly, he seems to believe that the Marxist theory of fascism simply reduces it to a stage army which the capitalist class can wheel out whenever it sees fit. Yet the contradictions he uncovers are accounted for precisely through Trotsky's analysis of the rise of fascism in Germany in the 1930s. He saw fascism's social base, among the 'petty bourgeoisie' driven mad by the crisis, not as a sociological label but as a key to explaining its appeal and weakness if faced with determined working class opposition. He captured its contradictory nature in a single phrase. He called fascism 'mass plebeian counter-revolution'. It was certainly counter-revolutionary—its leaders were committed to destroying the fighting capacity of the one class which could challenge capitalism, the working class. But unlike previous counter-revolutions which had been ushered in by the army from above, fascism was counter-revolution from below, from the middle classes. This accounted for its frenzy and the contradictions which made it unstable even when it came to power. Trotsky foresaw in 1933 the clash which eventually came in June 1934 between the Nazi leadership around Hitler and the Brownshirts who, taken in by the pseudo-revolutionary rhetoric, wanted to turn the Nazi seizure of power against private property.

The contradiction re-emerged after the 'Night of the Long Knives' in which Hitler liquidated the Brownshirts' leaders and, to a lesser extent, dealt with his bourgeois political opponents. It underpinned the anarchic competition between different branches of the Nazi Party and state machine which Kershaw rightly highlights. It partly explains the repeated crises Hitler faced even after he had smashed the working class by the summer of 1933.

There has been an enormous amount of historical research into the Nazis and the Third Reich since Trotsky wrote from exile on the island of Prikipo, relying on newspapers which were often three weeks late for information. This book and Kershaw's work generally are among the best of it. Like the bulk of writing on the period, it vindicates Trotsky's analysis even as it dismisses or remains ignorant of what he wrote. In so doing it reinforces the key message in what Trotsky had to say: Hitler could have been stopped.

Notes

1   I Kershaw, *Hitler 1889-1936: Hubris* (Allen Lane, 1998), p132.
2   Ibid, p320.
3   Ibid, p410.
4   Ibid, p327.
5   Ibid, p414.
6   Ibid, p425.
7   Ibid, p414.
8   Ibid, p424.
9   Ibid, p426.

The Socialist Workers Party is one of an international grouping of socialist organisations:

AUSTRALIA	International Socialists, PO Box A338, Sydney South
BRITAIN	Socialist Workers Party, PO Box 82, London E3
CANADA	International Socialists, PO Box 339, Station E, Toronto, Ontario M6H 4E3
CYPRUS	Ergatiki Demokratia, PO Box 7280, Nicosia
DENMARK	Internationale Socialister, Postboks 642, 2200 København N
GERMANY	Linksruck, Postfach 304 183, 20359 Hamburg
GREECE	Sosialistiko Ergatiko Komma, c/o Workers Solidarity, PO Box 8161, Athens 100 10
HOLLAND	Internationale Socialisten, PO Box 92052, 1090 AA Amsterdam
IRELAND	Socialist Workers Party, PO Box 1648, Dublin 8
NEW ZEALAND	Socialist Workers Organization, PO Box 8851, Auckland
NORWAY	Internasjonale Socialisterr, Postboks 9226 Grønland, 0134 Oslo
POLAND	Solidarność Socjalistyczna, PO Box 12, 01-900 Warszawa 118
SPAIN	Socialismo Internacional, Apartado 563, 08080, Barcelona
UNITED STATES	International Socialist Organisation, PO Box 16085, Chicago, Illinois 60616
ZIMBABWE	International Socialist Organisation, PO Box 6758, Harare

The following issues of *International Socialism* (second series) are available price £3 (including postage) from IS Journal, PO Box 82, London E3 3LH. *International Socialism* 2:58 and 2:65 are available on cassette from the Royal National Institute for the Blind (Peterborough Library Unit). Phone 01733 370777.

International Socialism 2:80 Autumn 1998
Clare Fermont: Indonesia: the inferno of revolution ★ Workers' representatives and socialists: Three interviews from Indonesia ★ Chris Bambery: Report from Indonesia ★ Tony Cliff: Revolution and counter-revolution: lessons for Indonesia ★ John Molyneux: The legitimacy of modern art ★ Gary McFarlane: A respectable trade? Slavery and the rise of capitalism ★ Paul McGarr: The French Revolution: Marxism versus capitalism ★ Shaun Doherty: Will the real James Connolly please stand up? ★

International Socialism 2:79 Summer 1998
John Rees: The return of Marx? ★ Lindsey German: Reflections on *The Communist Manifesto* ★ Judy Cox: An introduction to Marx's theory of alienation ★ Judith Orr: Making a comeback: the Marxist theory of crisis ★ Megan Trudell: New Labour, old conflicts: the story so far ★ John Molyneux: State of the art ★ Anna Chen: In perspective: Sergei Eisenstein ★ Jonathan Neale: Vietnam Veterans ★ Phil Gasper: Bookwatch: Marxism and science ★

International Socialism 2:78 Spring 1998
Colin Sparks: The eye of the storm ★ Shin Gyoung-hee: The crisis and the workers' movement in South Korea ★ Rob Hoveman: Financial crises and the real economy ★ Peter Morgan: Class divisions in the gay community ★ Alex Callinicos: The secret of the dialectic ★ John Parrington: It's life, Jim, but not as we know it ★ Judy Cox: Robin Hood: earl, outlaw or rebel? ★ Ian Birchall: The vice-like hold of nationalism? A comment on Megan Trudell's 'Prelude to revolution' ★ William Keach: In perspective: Alexander Cockburn and Christopher Hitchens ★

International Socialism 2:77 Winter 1997
Audrey Farrell: Addicted to profit—capitalism and drugs ★ Mike Gonzalez: The resurrections of Che Guevara ★ Sam Ashman: India: imperialism, partition and resistance ★ Henry Maitles: Never Again! ★ John Baxter: The return of political science ★ Dave Renton: Past its peak ★

International Socialism 2:76 Autumn 1997
Mike Haynes: Was there a parliamentary alternative in 1917? ★ Megan Trudell: Prelude to revolution: class consciousness and the First World War ★ Judy Cox: A light in the darkness ★ Pete Glatter: Victor Serge: writing for the future ★ Gill Hubbard: A guide to action ★ Chris Bambery: Review article: Labour's history of hope and despair ★

International Socialism 2:75 Summer 1997
John Rees: The class struggle under New Labour ★ Alex Callinicos: Europe: the mounting crisis ★ Lance Selfa: Mexico after the Zapatista uprising ★ William Keach: Rise like lions? Shelley and the revolutionary left ★ Judy Cox: What state are we really in? ★ John Parrington: In perspective: Valentin Voloshinov ★

International Socialism 2:74 Spring 1997
Colin Sparks: Tories, Labour and the crisis in education ★ Colin Wilson: The politics of information technology ★ Mike Gonzalez: No more heroes: Nicaragua 1996 ★ Christopher Hill: Tulmults and commotions: turning the world upside down ★ Peter Morgan: Capitalism without frontiers? ★ Alex Callinicos: Minds, machines and evolution ★ Anthony Arnove: In perspective: Noam Chomsky★

International Socialism 2:73 Winter 1996
Chris Harman: Globalisation: a critique of a new orthodoxy ★ Chris Bambery: Marxism and sport ★ John Parrington: Computers and consciousness: a reply to Alex Callinicos ★ Joe Faith: Dennett, materialism and empiricism ★ Megan Trudell: Who made the American Revolution? ★ Mark O'Brien: The class conflicts which shaped British history ★ John Newsinger: From class war to Cold War ★ Alex Callinicos: The state in debate ★ Charlie Kimber: Review article: coming to terms with barbarism in Rwanda in Burundi★

International Socialism 2:72 Autumn 1996
Alex Callinicos: Betrayal and discontent: Labour under Blair ★ Sue Cockerill and Colin Sparks: Japan in crisis ★ Richard Levins: When science fails us ★ Ian Birchall: The Babeuf bicentenary: conspiracy or revolutionary party? ★ Brian Manning: A voice for the poor ★ Paul O'Flinn: From the kingdom of necessity to the kingdom of freedom: Morris's *News from Nowhere* ★ Clare Fer-

International Socialism 2:59 Summer 1993
Ann Rogers: Back to the workhouse ★ Kevin Corr and Andy Brown: The labour aristocracy and the roots of reformism ★ Brian Manning: God, Hill and Marx ★ Henry Maitles: Cutting the wire: a criticial appraisal of Primo Levi ★ Hazel Croft: Bookwatch: women and work ★

International Socialism 2:58 Spring 1993
Chris Harman: Where is capitalism going? (part one) ★ Ruth Brown and Peter Morgan: Politics and the class struggle today: a roundtable discussion ★ Richard Greeman: The return of Comrade Tulayev: Victor Serge and the tragic vision of Stalinism ★ Norah Carlin: A new English revolution ★ John Charlton: Building a new world ★ Colin Barker: A reply to Dave McNally ★

International Socialism 2:56 Autumn 1992
Chris Harman: The Return of the National Question ★ Dave Treece: Why the Earth Summit failed ★ Mike Gonzalez: Can Castro survive? ★ Lee Humber and John Rees: The good old cause—an interview with Christopher Hill ★ Ernest Mandel: The Impasse of Schematic Dogmatism ★

International Socialism 2:55 Summer 1992
Alex Callinicos: Race and class ★ Lee Sustar: Racism and class struggle in the American Civil War era ★ Lindsey German and Peter Morgan: Prospects for socialists—an interview with Tony Cliff ★ Robert Service: Did Lenin lead to Stalin? ★ Samuel Farber: In defence of democratic revolutionary socialism ★ David Finkel: Defending 'October' or sectarian dogmatism? ★ Robin Blackburn: Reply to John Rees ★ John Rees: Dedicated followers of fashion ★ Colin Barker: In praise of custom ★ Sheila McGregor: Revolutionary witness ★

International Socialism 2:54 Spring 1992
Sharon Smith: Twilight of the American dream ★ Mike Haynes: Class and crisis—the transition in eastern Europe ★ Costas Kossis: A miracle without end? Japanese capitalism and the world economy ★ Alex Callinicos: Capitalism and the state system: A reply to Nigel Harris ★ Steven Rose: Do animals have rights? ★ John Charlton: Crime and class in the 18th century ★ John Rees: Revolution, reform and working class culture ★ Chris Harman: Blood simple ★

International Socialism 2:51 Summer 1991
Chris Harman: The state and capitalism today ★ Alex Callinicos: The end of nationalism? ★ Sharon Smith: Feminists for a strong state? ★ Colin Sparks and Sue Cockerill: Goodbye to the Swedish miracle ★ Simon Phillips: The South African Communist Party and the South African working class ★ John Brown: Class conflict and the crisis of feudalism ★

International Socialism 2:49 Winter 1990
Chris Bambery: The decline of the Western Communist Parties ★ Ernest Mandel: A theory which has not withstood the test of time ★ Chris Harman: Criticism which does not withstand the test of logic ★ Derek Howl: The law of value In the USSR ★ Terry Eagleton: Shakespeare and the class struggle ★ Lionel Sims: Rape and pre-state societies ★ Sheila McGregor: A reply to Lionel Sims ★

International Socialism 2:48 Autumn 1990
Lindsey German: The last days of Thatcher ★ John Rees: The new imperialism ★ Neil Davidson and Donny Gluckstein: Nationalism and the class struggle in Scotland ★ Paul McGarr: Order out of chaos ★

International Socialism 2:46 Winter 1989
Chris Harman: The storm breaks ★ Alex Callinicos: Can South Africa be reformed? ★ John Saville: Britain, the Marshall Plan and the Cold War ★ Sue Clegg: Against the stream ★ John Rees: The rising bourgeoisie ★

International Socialism 2:44 Autumn 1989
Charlie Hore: China: Tiananmen Square and after ★ Sue Clegg: Thatcher and the welfare state ★ John Molyneux: *Animal Farm* revisited ★ David Finkel: After Arias, is the revolution over? ★ John Rose: Jews in Poland ★

International Socialism 2:41 Winter 1988
Polish socialists speak out: Solidarity at the Crossroads ★ Mike Haynes: Nightmares of the market ★ Jack Robertson: Socialists and the unions ★ Andy Strouthous: Are the unions in decline? ★ Richard Bradbury: What is Post-Structuralism? ★ Colin Sparks: George Bernard Shaw ★

International Socialism 2:39 Summer 1988
Chris Harman and Andy Zebrowski: Glasnost, before the storm ★ Chanie Rosenberg: Labour and the fight against fascism ★ Mike Gonzalez: Central America after the Peace Plan ★ Ian Birchall: Raymond Williams ★ Alex Callinicos: Reply to John Rees ★